INCOTERMS AMERICANS®

(Completely Rewritten For Incoterms® 2010)

Simplifies and answers questions about Incoterms® 2010 rules for U.S. business.

by **Frank Reynolds**
with editorial assistance from
Margaret Gatti, Esq.
Patricia Skaff

from **INTERNATIONAL PROJECTS, INC.**

ISBN: 978-1-886457-11-9

Preface & Acknowledgements

This is the third version of Incoterms® for Americans®. It has been completely rewritten over the summer of 2010.

I suppose explaining the reason for two registered trademark symbols is a good place to start. The word "Incoterms" is a registered trademark of the Paris based International Chamber of Commerce (ICC), which has been providing and updating these trade rules since 1936. The phrase "Incoterms® for Americans®" belongs to my company, International Projects, Inc., and "Incoterms®" is used in it with ICC permission.

There are several reasons for this third revision. The most obvious is that the ICC replaced Incoterms 2000[i] with Incoterms® 2010[ii]. The second is that the shipment and delivery terms formerly found in §2.319 through §2.324 of the Uniform Commercial Code were deleted as part of a major overhaul in 2004. Third, the previous version of Incoterms for Americans® sold nearly ten thousand copies, which proves that it was somewhat useful in explaining how these terms really work from an American perspective. Finally, as I wrote in the last version, one learns a lot over ten years.

Having served as the U.S. delegate for the Incoterms 2000 revision, I had no concerns about fitting in this time, at least until I met the other Drafting Group members. With the exception of our capable ICC Moderator, Emily O'Connor, I was the only non-European. I was also the only non-lawyer, this time including Esq. O'Connor. Despite what could have been a serious handicap, things went very well. The other drafters showed a fair amount of deference to trade practice, even to the point of touring a seaport. Together, we were able to draft an improved up-to-date version. For this I owe a huge thank you to the drafting group co-chairs Charles Debattista (UK) and Christophe Martin Radke (France) as well as to my other Drafting Group colleagues:
Jens Bredow, Germany
Johnny Harre, Sweden
David Lowe, United Kingdom
Lauri Relais, Finland
Miroslav Subert, Czech Republic

We also had considerable help from ICC intern Shane Daly. Although as of this writing he is not yet fully in the lawyer camp, he's well on his way.

The aforementioned Emily O'Connor kept us on track, sometimes slapping our wrists and always humoring us along. She and Shane had the unenviable task of putting each draft together after we left. This meant keeping track of who said what, numerous side conversations, a few outbursts, and in the end determining exactly what had been decided. This is no easy task with eight outspoken drafters at ten drafting meetings addressing approximately two thousand comments submitted from thirty-plus countries over a two and a half year period.

Many thanks also to the ICC for:

1. inventing Incoterms® rules in 1936,
2. revising them as needed,
3. again inviting me to participate in the revision,
4. providing the official Incoterms®2010 publication and the Guide to Incoterms®2010[iii] to the trade,
5. realizing that this book is an American commentary and is not intended as a substitute for point 4.

As the ICC's U.S. affiliate organization, the United States Council for International Business serves as the local source for ICC products and services (www.uscib.org). It also operates ICC Publishing Inc., (www.iccbooksusa.com), the U.S. source for all ICC publications.

Margaret Gatti, Esq. of Dilworth Paxson LLP is a close friend and a very trade-savvy international lawyer. She provided not only the requested "keep me out of trouble" advice, but substantial help in developing clarity. If she didn't get something first time around, the problem was with the text, not the editor. Thank you, Margaret!

Patricia Skaff is another friend who both manages a foreign trade operation and instructs international trade related topics at Lourdes College. As I am doing less "hands-on" importing and exporting lately, she kept me down to earth with current information on the way things really work in practice. Thank you, Patti!

Kitty Callahan is my extremely supportive and patient soulmate. Fortunately for me, she is also my wife. Not only did she put up with the incessant travel and constant distraction this project caused, but frequently stepped in to run our normal business. Her keen sense of humor and genuine caring keeps me focused. So, Kitty, as with the previous two versions, this one's for you.

Frank Reynolds

Toledo, Ohio, August 16, 2010

---

[i] Incoterms 2000, (ISBN 92-842-1199-9), ICC No. 560, ICC Publishing SA, Paris, France, available from ICC Publishing Inc., New York, NY

[ii] Incoterms® 2010, (ISBN 978-92-842-0080-1), ICC No. 720, ICC Publishing SA, Paris, France, available from ICC Publishing Inc., New York, NY

[iii] Guide to Incoterms 2010®, (ISBN 978-92-842-0082-5), ICC No 720, Jan Ramberg, ICC Publishing SA, Paris, France, available from ICC Publishing Inc., NY, NY

General Introduction

The decision to revise Incoterms 2000[iv] was by no means unanimous. A number of International Chamber of Commerce (ICC) National Committees and Incoterms® experts gave some pretty convincing reasons to leave things as they were. However, led by Finland, Germany, Austria and the United States, the ICC's Commercial Law and Practice Commission finally voted for the revision in November 2007. A Drafting Group was appointed, and I was again selected to represent the U.S.

Nine drafting meetings followed, and the final (fourth) proposed draft was submitted to the Commercial Law and Practice Commission for approval on May 6, 2010. The rest is history, and the official Incoterms® 2010[v] was released the following September to come into force on 1/1/11. There was something irresistible about all those ones.

Once the decision to revise was made, everyone got on board. There are many improvements, and some of the most significant and best ones were made by the very same experts who initially opposed the revision.

The United States Council for International Business, ICC's U.S. affiliate, spearheaded the drive for revision for several reasons. The deletion of the old shipment and delivery terms from the Uniform Commercial Code in 2004 made Incoterms® rules an attractive replacement for U.S. domestic use. We wrote a book and ran some seminars on this in 2005, and some major companies expressed real interest. However, given the ten year history of Incoterms® revisions, people naturally wanted to wait for the brand new version before switching. A second U.S. obstacle was the lack of a duty-neutral term for domestic sales of pre-imported goods in Incoterms 2000. One could choose only between either DDU or the ever-dangerous DDP (which while appropriate for this limited situation could easily be misused elsewhere). This has been remedied by the introduction of DAP in Incoterms® 2010.

Another reason for the revision was a potentially dangerous vague area in CPT and CIP in Incoterms 2000. As with all "C-Group" Incoterms® rules, the seller delivers by handing the contract goods over to a carrier while paying the freight cost to the cited place. The fact that when subsequent carriers are used, the seller delivers at the first carrier in CPT and CIP was too often overlooked. This can expose buyers to unforeseen risk when pre-carriage is done independently of main carriage. We couldn't change the "first carrier" provision in the CPT and CIP rules, but did include adequate warnings for the parties to agree to both the delivery point and the place to which the seller pays for transportation.

There was one thing I really wanted to change but couldn't. Lawyers are trained to easily cross reference from one part to another of texts while mere mortals like this writer aren't. I was determined to eliminate or reduce the "daisy chain" presentation found in previous versions; where A4 references A3, B5 references A4, B6 references A3, A8 references A3 and so on. However, when I tried to do so, I found that this is really an effective shorthand. Replacing these cross references with words resulted in an unacceptable increase in word count. My fallback position was to present each Incoterm® rule on an 8 ½ x 11 page by itself, at least for training purposes. This suggestion was refused by the powers that be, so keep a stack of sticky notes handy when first reading Incoterms® 2010.

As it turned out, the U.S. concerns were relatively conservative. There are about 92 ICC National Committees, and we heard from nearly half of them during the revision. All told there were over two thousand comments. Many covered the same problems like use of the old maritime rules for containerized transport (which we solved). Some wanted new rules for particular situations. Others had insurance issues like maximum cover as the default for CIF and CIP (we couldn't help but did warn) or insurance obligations in F-Group rules (again couldn't help). We were also informed of a number of inconsistencies in Incoterms 2000, which I'm embarrassed to admit were really there. (We found a way to reduce if not eliminate these for the Incoterms® 2010 rules.)

We'll summarize the changes in detail in Chapter Two. You will also see them in our coverage of each rule.

Readers familiar with Incoterms® will notice that we now frequently refer to them as "rules" rather than "terms." You will find the same treatment in the official Incoterms® 2010 and the Guide to Incoterms®2010[vi]. This is intentional, in order to convey the notion of "Incoterms® rules," as it doesn't make much sense to say "Incoterms® terms". Result is that FOB, CIF and all others are now called Incoterms® rules rather than terms. You will also see the copyright circled R symbol every time the word Incoterms® is used. The ICC is very interested in proclaiming that this word is a registered trademark in a number of countries.

In reviewing the problems encountered by users of previous versions, we learned that a disturbing number of people failed to read the Introduction and missed a good deal of information. For instance, in Incoterms 2000 that's where you find that Incoterms® *do not* address title transfer or breach of contract. (Care to guess how many title-related questions I've received over the past ten years?) For this reason, Incoterms® 2010 has a much shorter Introduction *which you had better read, as that's where the new definitions are*. We've moved much of the introductory information to a new feature called Guidance Notes which accompany each rule.

Now for some important caveats. As the title implies, this book is intended to explain Incoterms® 2010 rules in clear American business English to readers here and to those who frequently do business with us. It is NOT a substitute for the official ICC Incoterms® 2010. I suggest – no, insist – that you use these together. It is also not offered as a substitute for the detailed ICC Guide to Incoterms®2010, written by Professor Jan Ramberg who is probably the greatest living authority on the subject. Finally, alone among the Drafting Group members, I am not a lawyer, and nothing in this book is to be considered legal advice.

Realizing the widespread tendency to skip introductions, we'll end this one here, with the hope that you will read the following brief Instructions Chapter. It's only one page long!

Frank Reynolds

[iv] Incoterms 2000, (ISBN 92-842-1199-9), ICC No 560, ICC Publishing SA, Paris, France, available from ICC Publishing Inc., NY, NY

[v] Incoterms® 2010, (ISBN 978-92-842-0080-1), ICC No. 720, ICC Publishing SA, Paris, France, available from ICC Publishing Inc., New York, NY

[vi] Guide to Incoterms® 2010, (ISBN 978-92-842-0082-5), ICC No. 720, Jan Ramberg, ICC Publishing SA, Paris, France, available from ICC Publishing Inc., NY, NY

Instructions on How to Use this Book

This book is designed to be read cover-to-cover. Even those already experienced in subtopics like contract formation - yes, you lawyers - should do so. If nothing else, reading about a familiar topic will demonstrate the basic level at which this is written, which will enable you to accordingly interpret topics with which you are less familiar. As my part of the bargain, most of the book is deliberately written in small, easily digestible chapters.

Incoterms® 2010[vii] is also intended to be read cover-to-cover. The reason is that much can be gained from comparing the Incoterms® rules to each other. Also, reading the now smaller Incoterms® 2010 Introduction is a must. It will really help you use the new layout to your advantage.

Recognize that this book is a commentary. It is designed for use *with* and *not instead of* Incoterms® 2010. In fact, for best results you should have both books handy when reading either.

Why bother reading this book? Incoterms® rules are written for general use in all countries. Some rules work better than others in the U.S., and this is where this book can help. Further, the Incoterms® rules are written in British English and in a more or less lawyerly manner. I can help you clear these obstacles as well, as I was part of the drafting process and can convey what these rules mean in clear American business English. I have been exporting and importing for nearly fifty years, and know how trade really works as opposed to theory. Finally, I have been instructing Incoterms® for well over twenty years, and know what issues people find difficult to grasp. While this book brings all these assets to the party, only Incoterms® 2010 contains the official rules.

Don't try to use each and every Incoterms® rule. Only the largest users will find all eleven useful. Chances are, there are four or five you will be using most often. If you have followed my suggestions and have finished reading through this book and Incoterms®2010, go back to those rules that are of most immediate interest and reread them in both books.

A final point, be careful with visual aids like wall charts. Incoterms® rules are difficult to illustrate in two dimensions. While well intended, charts often contain errors. Since they are frequently "borrowed" from existing versions, errors can proliferate and come at you from several normally reliable sources. I've seen a train of the same error copied from one Incoterms 2000 wall chart version to another. My point is, you can't absorb an Incoterm® rule at a glance without first knowing how it works. Sadly, the people who rely most on visual aids are often the ones lacking this required detailed knowledge. The good news is that each rule in Incoterms® 2010 is accompanied by an illustration showing its typical use, thereby providing the visual aid and the text together.

[vii] Incoterms® 2010, (ISBN 978-92-842-0080-1), ICC No. 720, ICC Publishing SA, Paris, France, available from ICC Publishing Inc., New York, NY

PART I - HISTORY

Chapter 1 - Developments Outside Incoterms® Rules

Incoterms® rules are and have always been intended to reflect trade practice, not establish it. For this reason, developments having little or no direct impact on Incoterms® rules can require a new revision. Fortunately, as Incoterms® rules are not law, they may be revised any time the International Chamber of Commerce determines the need. This it can do with national committees in over ninety countries and some less formal affiliations in many more. The most recent decision to revise was taken in 2007, and Incoterms® 2010[viii] is the result.

Although titled Incoterms 2000[ix], the previous version was actually completed and released in 1999. The following is a short list of some of the many things that have changed since then.

- The Foreign Trade Statistical Regulations (FTSR) were revised, creating "Routed Exports" and thereby switching the reporting requirements from sellers to buyers whenever buyer-appointed forwarders are used. Although Census doesn't use Incoterms® rules, this refers to the EXW, FCA, FAS and FOB rules where the buyer handles main carriage.
- Required treatment and stamping for softwood pallets.
- 9/11.
- The Customs & Border Protection 24 hour rule imposed pre-loading reporting requirements on carriers for inbound containerized vessel shipments, while the Container Security Initiative (CSI) provided for container screening and inspection at major cooperating overseas ports.
- Known Shipper air freight requirements.
- Securities scandals and Sarbanes-Oxley brought increased attention to the timing for revenue and expense recognition, particularly by publicly traded U.S. corporations.
- U.S. importers tightened their supply chains and adopted voluntary control programs (C-TPAT).
- The 2004 Revision of Article Two of the Uniform Commercial Code (UCC) deleted the UCC's shipment and delivery terms (§2-319 through §2-324) as obsolete and no defined replacement was either enacted or suggested.
- The FTSR was again revised as the Foreign Trade Regulations (FTR) effective October 2008, retaining the Routed Export concept, requiring Electronic Export Information (EEI) reporting, and setting pre-shipment export reporting deadlines.
- Widespread imports of tainted goods (food containing melamine, lead painted toys, etc.) resulted in ongoing rounds of enhanced Consumer Product Safety Commission regulations.
- The 2008 Farm Bill's amendments to the Lacey Act imposed substantial new regulations and reporting requirements for imports of plants and plant derivatives.
- The Importer Security Filing and Additional Carrier Requirements (10+2) imposed additional pre-loading and increased data reporting requirements for a significant portion of waterborne imports, this time on both importers and carriers.
- In 2010 President Obama proclaimed a targeted doubling of U.S. exports over five years.
- The 9/11 Commission Act required 100 percent cargo inspection for all passenger flights and allowed for the development of certified cargo screening facilities.

These events are just what happened in the U.S. The euro (2002), and increased EU membership (2004), created an increasingly integrated expanded European "domestic market." China joined the World Trade Organization in 2001, replacing Germany as the world's biggest exporter by 2010. Nations developed their own cargo security procedures, often roughly similar yet different enough to limit widespread reciprocity. Retaliatory tariffs were imposed by a number of countries involving the United States (Byrd Amendment – EU, cross border trucking – Mexico, cotton – Brazil, etc.). The great recession shrunk trade worldwide, forcing carriers to lay up vessels and reduce service.

It was against this background that we worked on the 2010 revision. Incoterms® rules cannot possibly deal with all these situations, nor should they attempt to do so. They are merely shipment and delivery terms that also allocate certain tasks and associated costs to sellers and buyers. However, they can at least remind the parties that there are certain issues like export/import clearance and cargo security that must be addressed. Further, they can change existing rules and create new ones to facilitate situations like increased use in "quasi-domestic" trade within the EU and actual domestic use here. Finally, they can also contain a little built-in flexibility to address unanticipated major future developments.

Generally, lawyers prefer flexibility, bankers favor precision, while some traders would welcome a new rule for every conceivable trading situation. In the end, no one was completely satisfied with the revision, which indicates to me that we did a reasonably good job. We'll know for sure once they become generally used.

[viii] Incoterms® 2010, (ISBN 978-92-842-0080-1), ICC No. 720, ICC Publishing SA, Paris, France, available from ICC Publishing Inc., New York, NY
[ix] Incoterms 2000, (ISBN 92-842-1199-9), ICC No 560, ICC Publishing SA, Paris, France, available from ICC Publishing Inc., NY, NY

Chapter 2 - Summary of Major Changes

There are so many changes in Incoterms® 2010[x] from previous versions that we lost track of the number. I am willing to bet that there are hundreds. It is impossible to cover each change in a book of this kind but the following lists the most important ones. We'll divide them into presentation changes and individual rule changes to better keep track of them.

PRESENTATION CHANGES

Introduction

The Introduction was significantly reduced as we realized that too many readers were skipping the important information it contained. The now shorter version contains such vitally important topics as how to use the rules, main features of the new rules, variations from the rules, definitions, place specificity and caveats. It absolutely cannot be overlooked.

The Introduction explains that it is just that, and not part of the official text of each rule which is found in the matching columns (the so-called "black letter text").

Division

Incoterms®2010 is divided into two parts in order to strongly differentiate between the omnimodal rules and those used only for transport by vessel. The first part, omnimodal, includes EXW, FCA, CPT, CIP, DAT, DAP and DDP while the second includes the four remaining marine-only terms: FAS, FOB, CFR and CIF. The Introduction explains that the omnimodal terms may be and often are used for vessel shipments, while the marine-only terms are restricted to vessel shipments.

Within each part the rules are listed in increasing responsibility and cost for the seller. For this reason, the omnimodal part begins with EXW and runs through DDP while the marine-only part begins with FAS and runs through CIF.

While this new presentation clearly distinguishes between omnimodal and marine-only rules, it breaks the long held across-the-board progression from the least seller responsibility (EXW) to the greatest (DDP). The new lineup is as follows:

Omnimodal:

- Ex Works (EXW)
- Free Carrier (FCA)
- Carriage Paid To (CPT)
- Carriage and Insurance Paid To (CIP)
- Delivered At Terminal (DAT)
- Delivered At Place (DAP)
- Delivered Duty Paid (DDP)

Waterborne only:

- Free Alongside Ship (FAS)
- Free On Board (FOB)
- Cost and Freight (CFR)
- Cost Insurance and Freight (CIF)

Guidance Notes
Each rule is preceded by useful notes that explain when and how to use it. Some of these pointers were formerly found in the Incoterms 2000[xi] Introduction, while others are intended to alert the reader to a situation particular to the rule with which they are found. Our hope is that locating these so close to the matching columns will entice even a casual reader to read them.

As with the Introduction, the Guidance Notes are not part of the official rule.

Illustrations
Each rule will have an illustration showing its typical use.

Task Headings
While there are still ten task rows (A1-A10 and B1-B10) for each rule, some heading titles have been changed from Incoterms 2000.

Export Clearance and Import Clearance
The phrase "where applicable" has been frequently used to stress the fact that the Incoterms® 2010 rules may be used for domestic as well as international transactions.

"No Obligation"
Situations where one party has no obligation to the other, such as insurance in all rules except CIP and CIF.

Point versus Place
The importance of clearly specifying a point within a place has been stressed frequently throughout the rules.

Cargo Security
A10-B10 of all rules and A2 of EXW specifically speak to exchanges of required cargo security information. We needed to keep these flexible because of the differences in security regulations different countries impose, and the fact that these regulations are constantly changing.

Provision for "String Sales"
A3 of the CFR and CIF rules now obligate the seller to either contract for carriage or obtain a freight prepaid carriage contract for goods already shipped. A4 of FAS, FOB, CFR and CIF also mentions the possibility of sellers providing goods delivered by others. These are to address situations where the original buyer resells the goods after vessel loading or while they are in transit, as frequently happens in commodity trade.

Container Loading
The definition of packaging specifically excludes container loading from Incoterms® 2010 rules. Sellers and buyers should specify this task elsewhere in their contracts.

CHANGES TO INDIVIDUAL RULES

Deletions and Innovations

The former Incoterms 2000 Delivered At Frontier (DAF), Delivered Ex Ship (DES), Delivered Ex Quay (DEQ) and Delivered Duty Unpaid (DDU) rules have been deleted. Two new rules were added: Delivered At Place (DAP) and Delivered At Terminal (DAT). The following will explain how and why.

Delivered at Place (DAP) replaces DAF, DES and DDU.

DAF was an omnimodal rule that held the seller responsible for the condition of the goods and all transportation costs to the agreed place on the agreed border. When used at all, it was largely for shipments made entirely by ground. Any other use was restricted to situations where at least the last transportation leg was on the ground. It was rarely used in practice, as actual border transfer points are seldom at the physical borders, and there are other more commonly used alternatives available.

DES was a marine-only rule that held the seller responsible for the condition of the contract goods and all transportation costs until the arrival of the carrying vessel at the agreed port, before unloading. Its marine-restricted nature and the fact that it did not speak to unloading largely limited its use to voyage charter vessel shipments, as liner carriers usually load and unload their own vessels.

DDU was omnimodal and used for arrival contracts where the seller bears responsibility for the condition of the contract goods and all transportation costs until they arrive at the agreed place. This term was widely used. Its only flaw was its name, Delivered Duty Unpaid, which implied that a) there was duty and b) that it wasn't paid. This hampered its use in domestic transactions, particularly those involving pre-cleared imported goods for which duty had already been paid. The only other omnimodal arrival contract rule, Delivered Duty Paid, correctly indicated that duty had already been paid, and is appropriate for pre-imported goods. However, DDP is so dangerous that its frequent use in domestic transactions could easily lead to its inadvertent use in international transactions by people unfamiliar with the consequences. Therefore, we replaced it with the "duty-neutral" DAP.

DAP resolves all these limitations. It may be used for arrival contracts with a border location or aboard a vessel, or a port location, or just about anywhere else. Also, its name says nothing about duty one way or the other. The default position is duty unpaid if applicable, and of course there wouldn't be any further duty for foreign made goods that have already been cleared for import, or any duty at all on domestically produced goods.

An omnimodal, duty neutral rule for use in both international and domestic arrival contracts was a major U.S. request, and we now have a good one. I tried to name it "Delivered At Destination," but couldn't sell the other drafters on "DAD."

The Guidance Notes caution the parties to specify the agreed destination as clearly as possible, and that the seller contract for carriage to that exact point. The buyer is not obligated to reimburse the seller for any additional costs for carriage beyond that point. This is to prevent a situation where both the seller and buyer are billed for such arrival costs as unloading.

Delivered At Terminal (DAT) replaces DEQ

DEQ was a marine-only rule that held the seller responsible for the condition of the contract goods and all transportation costs until they were placed on the quay at the agreed port. Its marine-restricted nature and the fact that container carriers usually remove unloaded containers to their terminals and container yards largely limited its use to charter vessel shipments.

In our first draft, we decided to eliminate DEQ along with DES. However, doing so would leave us with no Incoterms® rule requiring the seller to unload, which would present a problem when the seller's contract of carriage includes unloading. (For instance, large project cargo transported on geared "self unloading" vessels.) As the new DAP rule tasks the buyer with unloading, it would not be a suitable replacement for DEQ, so we reinstated DEQ in our second draft. However, this did nothing for containerized shipments where the carrier typically unloads and removes the containers to its terminal or container yard. Toward the end of the revision, several national committees suggested that we replace DEQ with an omnimodal rule tasking the seller with unloading for use in arrival contracts, thus DAT was devised. This accommodates DEQ situations as the parties can simply make the agreed place a quay at a destination port. It also works for all manner of transportation when the parties agree to make the seller responsible for unloading and moving the goods from the conveyance to a terminal, container yard, etc.

Ex Works (EXW) Warnings

We placed strong warnings about the problems with using the EXW rule for international transactions. The fact that the buyer has only limited obligations to provide information that the seller may need has been stressed.

Free Carrier (FCA)

FCA is the specifically recommended rule for international transactions where the parties want the seller's obligations to be at a minimum.

Carriage Paid To (CPT)

There are several important changes to this omnimodal rule for use in freight-prepaid shipment contracts.

It is often the case in multimodal transportation that there is more than one carrier. The CPT Incoterms® rule specifies that the seller delivers at the first carrier unless the parties agree otherwise. This means that the seller's risk for the condition of the contract goods ends at the first carrier. This can be particularly risky for the buyer if the contract of carriage is not on a "door-to- somewhere" (door, port, airport, etc.) basis, so that the first carrier operates independently of the main carrier. For instance, in a port-to-port contract of main carriage, a small independent trucking company which is not part of the main carriage contract damages or loses the goods en-route to the main carrier. The buyer cannot claim on the main carrier as the problem occurred before the shipment arrived there. The result could therefore be the buyer's needing to claim on a small trucking company in a foreign country. The Guidance Notes clearly warn about this, and recommend that the parties consider both the place of delivery and the place of destination.

The Guidance Notes further caution the parties to specify the agreed destination as clearly as possible, and that the seller contract for carriage to that exact point. The buyer is not obligated to reimburse the seller for any additional costs for carriage beyond that point. This is to prevent a situation where both the seller and buyer are billed for such arrival costs as unloading.

Carriage and Insurance Paid To (CIP)

Please refer to the above CPT comments which also apply to CIP. Both the Guidance Notes and A3 caution that the default position is minimum cover (Clauses C). However, for the first time, A3 mentions by name the possibility of extended cover (Clauses A or B) as well as the War Clauses and Strike Clauses mentioned in previous Incoterms® versions. The "first carrier" risk is obviously lessened if the CIP seller exceeds the default obligation and provides extended cover insurance.

Delivered Duty Paid (DDP)
The Guidance Notes caution the parties to specify the agreed destination as clearly as possible, and that the seller contract for carriage to that exact point. The buyer is not obligated to reimburse the seller for any additional costs for carriage beyond that point. This is to prevent a situation where both the seller and buyer are billed for such arrival costs as unloading.

Free Alongside Ship (FAS)
The Guidance Notes clearly warn that this rule is inappropriate for containerized shipments. Both the Guidance Notes and A4 mention the possibility of the seller providing goods that have already been delivered to address string sales.

Free On Board (FOB)
The Guidance Notes clearly warn that this rule is inappropriate for containerized shipments. Both the Guidance Notes and A4 mention the possibility of the seller providing goods that have already been delivered to address string sales. The phrase "ship's rail," formerly included in the preamble of FOB in Incoterms 2000, does not appear in the FOB guidance notes. This increases the seller's risk, since no longer is it sufficient for the goods to merely cross the ship's rail. Now they must be loaded, and this could have different meanings depending on the type of vessel and the nature of the cargo. The parties are strongly advised to agree about exactly what "loading" entails elsewhere in their contract.

Cost and Freight (CFR)
The Guidance Notes clearly warn that this rule is inappropriate for containerized shipments. Both the Guidance Notes and A4 mention the possibility of the seller providing goods that have already been delivered to address string sales. The phrase "ship's rail," formerly included in the preamble of CFR in Incoterms 2000, does not appear in the CFR guidance notes. This increases the seller's risk, since no longer is it sufficient for the goods to merely cross the ship's rail. Now they must be loaded, and this could have different meanings depending on the type of vessel and the nature of the cargo. The parties are strongly advised to agree about exactly what "loading" entails elsewhere in their contract. The Guidance Notes further caution the parties to specify the agreed destination as clearly as possible, and that the seller contract for carriage to that exact point. The buyer is not obligated to reimburse the seller for any additional costs for carriage beyond that point. This is to prevent a situation where both the seller and buyer are billed for such arrival costs as unloading.

Cost Insurance and Freight (CIF)
Please refer to the above CFR comments which also apply to CIF. Both the Guidance Notes and A3 caution that the default position is minimum cover (Clauses C). However, for the first time, A3 mentions by name the possibility of extended cover (Clauses A or B) as well as the War Clauses and Strike Clauses mentioned in previous Incoterms® versions.

---

[x] Incoterms® 2010, (ISBN 978-92-842-0080-1), ICC No. 720, ICC Publishing SA, Paris, France, available from ICC Publishing Inc., New York, NY
[xi] Incoterms 2000, (ISBN 92-842-1199-9), ICC No 560, ICC Publishing SA, Paris, France, available from ICC Publishing Inc., NY, NY

PART II – BASIC CONCEPTS

Chapter 3 - Some Useful Definitions

The Introduction of Incoterms® 2010[xii] has a definition section. I suggest you go there right now and read these. This new feature did not come easily, and is the result of continued insistence on the part of several revision participants including this writer.

One of the reasons why some experts were reluctant to provide definitions is that the same word or phrase could have a number of different meanings in different contexts. "Delivery" is one such word. As the cautious lawyers participating in the revision pointed out, it can have different meanings in different kinds of law (contract, transport, etc.) For my part, it was enough to stipulate the definition to the way it is used in the Incoterms® rules, which is the point where the seller ceases to be responsible for the condition of the contract goods. This is a very important concept, and is covered in A4-B4 of every Incoterms® 2010 rule. The problem I see is that for at least American English speakers, the word delivery normally means arrival in everyday speech. ("The letter was delivered yesterday.") This dual use can make the C-Group Incoterms® rules difficult to grasp, as the seller delivers at shipment rather than arrival at the place accompanying the rule.

Since this is not an official ICC publication, and is written primarily for American readers, I am going beyond Incoterms® 2010 by defining additional terms that I think are useful for us. These are very much informal layman's definitions reflecting American usage. I have written a dictionary for the ICC, and have experience when it comes to defining terms, but remind you that I am not a lawyer.

We'll classify them by subject matter.

Transportation related

- **Carrier** - a party undertaking transportation responsibilities. Carriers may be performing like ship lines and airlines, or a non-performing like Non Vessel Operating Common Carriers (NVOCCs).
- **Contract of carriage**: a contract covering transportation between someone and a carrier. (See, this isn't rocket science!)
- **Pre-carriage**: transportation on the seller's side of main carriage (from the place where the shipment originates to the port, airport or border point where it leaves the seller's side). We Americans call this "inland freight" or more precisely "inland freight on the seller's side."
  Note: Tasks A3-B3 of FCA (+ a place other than the seller's premises), FAS and FOB specify that the seller has no obligation to contract for carriage. This is technically correct, as with these Incoterms® 2010 rules the seller delivers at the named place other than its own premises, or alongside a ship, or on board a ship. However, the seller is obligated to get the goods to the point of delivery, and unless the shipment originates there some pre-carriage is required. So, when considering "carriage" in A3 of these terms keep in mind that they mean the seller has no main carriage obligation but will need to handle pre-carriage.
- **Main carriage**: transportation from the seller's side to the buyer's side.
- **On-carriage**: transportation from the arrival point on the buyer's side to any other place on the buyer's side (such as to the buyer's premises). We Americans would call this "inland freight on buyer's side," which is an excellent reason to use the terms "pre-carriage" and "on-carriage" instead of two different "inland freights."

It's easy to define "seller's side" and "buyer's side" in international transactions, as the seller's side would normally be the seller's country while the buyer's side would normally be the buyer's country. It's not as obvious with domestic transactions as both parties are in the same country. However, for both international and domestic transactions, we can specify the "seller's side" as the seller's side of main carriage and the "buyer's side" as the buyer's side of main carriage. If there's only one carriage, the problem disappears entirely.

- Door-to-door: A single contract of carriage that includes pre-carriage + main carriage + on-carriage, which is all the carriage there is. (Think integrated small package carrier.)
- Door-to-port (or door-to-airport): A single contract of carriage that includes pre-carriage + main carriage. Someone else has to handle any necessary on-carriage.
- Port (or airport)-to-port (or airport): A contract of carriage that covers main carriage only. Someone else must handle any necessary pre-carriage and/or on-carriage. (Think oversized cargo shipped by vessel.)
- Port (or airport)-to door: A contract of carriage that includes main carriage and on-carriage. Someone else must handle any necessary pre-carriage.
- On-board: A marine transport document bearing the phrase "on board" or its equivalent and indicating the date that the goods were physically laden on the carrying vessel.
- Received for shipment: A transport document evidencing that a named carrier has received the described goods for shipment. Although it may indicate the name of the vessel or flight numbers, this document is often issued prior to actual transport.

Incoterms® rules related

- Omnimodal: Those Incoterms® rules that can be used for all transport modes (EXW, FCA, CPT, CIP, DAT, DAP and DDP). To my knowledge, I invented this word and provided something approaching official status by including it in the ICC's dictionary, A to Z of International Trade.[xiii]
- Marine-restricted: Those Incoterms® rules (FAS, FOB, CFR, CIF) that can be used only for vessel shipments.

Insurance related

- Minimum cover: Cargo insurance that covers only minimum perils, often called "Free of Particular Average (FPA)" in the United States, and "Institute Cargo Clauses C" (LMA/IUA) internationally. This is the default insurance position for the CIP and CIF Incoterms® rules.
- All risk: An inaccurate American term for cargo insurance coverage that is adequate for most shipments when written on a warehouse-to-warehouse basis and if it is enhanced with "War" and "Strike, Riot and Civil Commotion (SRCC)" coverages. (We should really call this "almost all risks," as war and strike coverage must normally be purchased separately as additional risks.) The more correct internationally recognized term is "Institute Cargo Clauses A" (LMA/IUA), and where necessary this should be enhanced by "Institute War and Strike Clauses" (LMA/IUA) or equivalent.

Contract related

- **Shipment contract**: a sales contact holding the seller responsible for the condition of the contract goods until they are handed over to a carrier or other named party for transportation. The Incoterms® rules used in shipment contracts are the F-Group and the C-Group. (With EXW, the seller delivers by merely having the goods available.)
- **Arrival contract**: a sales contact holding the seller responsible for the condition of the contract goods until they arrive at an agreed place. The D-Group Incoterms® rules are used in arrival contracts. (Arrival contracts are also sometimes called "destination contracts." We will not do so in this book, as Incoterms®2010 in some places uses destination to mean merely the place to which freight costs are paid.)
- **Title**: Incoterms® rules do not address the passage of title, and the parties are encouraged to agree to this elsewhere in the sales contract. For contracts that are silent and are governed by

the law of a U.S. state (with the possible exception of Louisiana), title is normally addressed by that state's version of the Uniform Commercial Code §2.401. (I use the word "normally" as I am not a lawyer and as there are other issues like liens and security interests which go far beyond the scope of this book.) Incidentally, the United Nations Convention on Contracts for the International Sale of Goods (CISG) under which significant international business is transacted is silent about ownership transfer.

Accounting related

- **Revenue recognition**: There are rules that determine when a sale becomes an account receivable. (Think: when can you ring the cash register.)

[xii] Incoterms® 2010, (ISBN 978-92-842-0080-1), ICC No. 720, ICC Publishing SA, Paris, France, available from ICC Publishing Inc., New York, NY

[xiii] A to Z of International Trade, ISBN 92 842 1277 4, ICC No. 623, Frank Reynolds, ICC Publishing SA, Paris, France, page 143, available from ICC Publishing Inc., New York, NY

Chapter 4 - Role of Incoterms® Rules in Sales Contracts

Nothing is more basic to successful repeat business than a meeting of the minds between seller and buyer.

At first this sounds about as exciting as kissing your sibling, but think about it for a while. After all, where do most commercial problems start: misunderstanding! - misunderstanding between sellers and buyers, between sellers and their own factories, between either party and carriers. For international transactions, add the potential for misunderstanding between exporters and their freight forwarders, importers and their customs brokers, banks and everyone else, and failure to observe applicable government regulations.

Throughout this book we are considering business-to-business sales and purchases of tangible, portable goods. For economy of words, we will refer to such transactions as "sales contracts," although buyers would be as likely to call them "purchase contracts." Regardless of which you call them, they are contracts between sellers and buyers.

Before we go further, I want to again call your attention to the fact that I am not a lawyer. Nothing in this book should be considered legal advice. Rather, it is the practical recommendations of an experienced international trader.

Incoterms® rules were developed for international trade where there is tremendous potential for uncertainty. By definition, goods pass from one country to another. This often involves different languages, different business norms, different cultures, different standards, different currencies with changing exchange rates, and two or more different bodies of law. Sellers and buyers are often located further apart than is true for domestic business, often in very different time zones. Greater distance usually means higher transportation costs, making returns of incorrect goods very costly. Also, with transport by sea, weeks may pass after shipment before anyone becomes aware that a problem exists.

The potential for confusion is not limited to international transactions. For many years, we Americans have been using the shipment and delivery terms that were found in §2-319 through §2-324 of the Uniform Commercial Code (UCC). These terms were never easy to understand, particularly as everyone's favorite - FOB - morphed into versions for use in both shipment and arrival contracts for both freight prepaid and freight collect situations. We thought we knew what we were doing, and likely knew what we wanted to happen, until controversy occurred which often brought surprises to one or both parties. This is probably a major reason these terms were deleted from the UCC as obsolete in 2004. However, contract law is state rather than federal, and it is likely to take some time before these UCC revisions are adopted by all the states, adding to the confusion potential.

Readers involved in both international and domestic business realize the inconvenience of using

Incoterms® rules for international trade and the old UCC terms domestically. For this reason, there is likely to be a shift towards the domestic use of Incoterms® rules as larger companies standardize around them for all transactions. This may well mirror the ripple effect that introduced e-commerce, when major companies insisted that their suppliers communicate with them electronically, causing the suppliers to require the same of their own vendors, and so on.

TERMS OF SHIPMENT AND DELIVERY IN SALES CONTRACTS

There are more contracts involved in business-to-business sales transactions than meet the eye. Someone must provide for non-product services to get the contract goods into the buyer's hands. We ship so often that we can lose sight of the fact that every shipment is actually a contract of carriage between someone (seller or buyer) and a carrier. One also hopes that someone is arranging for insurance to cover the goods in transit, and this is another contract.

Shipment and delivery terms such as Incoterms® rules answer the questions "who does what" and "who pays for what" by tasking the parties. This usually means one party or the other providing non-product services like transportation and insurance. Whoever does so is normally in a position of selecting and contracting with the service providers, and providing instructions as part of these contracts. The contracting party is therefore in a position to exert more control over the service provider than is the other party.

Carrier and forwarder selection are particularly important in international trade, where open account payment terms are less common than in domestic business. Some frequently used payment terms like documentary letters of credit and documentary collections require correctly executed documentation to work properly. Some critically important documents are prepared by forwarders and carriers, so selection of these service providers is an important payment term consideration. It makes little sense for a seller to insist on a documentary credit without the ability to instruct these service providers about the preparation and disposition of the required documents. This should logically lead sellers relying on accurate documentation for payment purposes toward those Incoterms® rules that task them with providing main carriage transportation – the C-Group and D-Group.

In Incoterms® 2010[xiv], as with previous versions, only two rules speak to insurance - CIP and CIF. All other rules are silent. Both CIP and CIF require the seller to provide insurance, but sellers may satisfy this obligation by providing only minimum cover. This is not to say that no insurance is required for the other rules, or that minimum cover is preferred. Far from it. It is only that there are practical considerations which dictate that for the other rules, the parties are best served by deciding who should insure elsewhere in the sales contract. Also, even for CIP and CIF, the desired level of coverage should be agreed separately from the Incoterms® rule.

There are numerous government regulations that require compliance. All trade, even domestic, is regulated for hazardous materials and consumer product safety. International regulations are far more complex. All countries have some sort of import clearance regulations, and the U.S. has what are probably the most demanding export regulations of any free world nation. There are also country-specific product standards like the EU CE Mark and Mexican NOMS, and environmentally driven rules like the Lacey Act. Meanwhile, cargo security concerns have brought a seemingly endless series of regulations in the post 9/11 world. Once again, Incoterms® rules answer the question "who does what," by assigning such tasks as export and import clearance and cargo security information to sellers and buyers.

OTHER SALES CONTRACT CONSIDERATIONS

Important as shipment and delivery terms are, they do not address all issues in a sales contract. It is important that sellers and buyers clearly agree on what they want to happen. Failure to do so can lead to disputes that in turn can result in arbitration or litigation. If contracts are silent about important issues, the governing law will likely impose its own "gap-fillers." This can have surprising results.

Since Americans and many other people enjoy pretty broad contractual freedom, it is best to specify whatever you believe important in your contract. The following checklist may be helpful.

- identities and addresses of seller and buyer
- description of items exchanged (goods and/or services) and pricing
- terms of shipment and delivery, preferably using an Incoterms® rule
- place of shipment and/or delivery and/or arrival
- terms of payment
- passage of title
- timeline for performance
- applicable law
- dispute resolution method and procedures
- names and capacities of signatories.

Failure to specify these in the contract can lead to some strange "gap-filler" results from the UCC. Here are a few samples: If a contract is silent about when payment is due, the default position is that it will be at the point where the buyer is to receive the goods (UCC §2-310). If the place is not specified, the default position is that it will be at the seller's place of business (UCC §2-308). If the manner of delivery is not specified, the default position is that it will be a single shipment (UCC §2-307). If title passage is not specified, it will be when the seller "delivers" (UCC §2-401). It may well be that neither of the parties had anything like these in mind when entering into the agreement. One of the nice things about Incoterms® rules is that they practically force the parties to consider most of these important issues.

Insurance is another important consideration that sellers and buyers should address in their contracts.

WHAT INCOTERMS® RULES BRING TO SALES CONTRACTS

As well defined shipment and delivery terms, Incoterms® rules bring certain benefits to business-to-business contracts for the sale/purchase of tangible, portable goods.

- They come from the private sector International Chamber of Commerce (ICC) rather than law. This means that they reflect trade practice rather than attempting to legislate it. It also means that they can be revised to reflect changes in trade practice, and since 1980 this has been done about every ten years.
- They have been used in international trade for many years and are widely understood worldwide. The first version was released in 1936 and the previous version, Incoterms 2000[xv], has been translated into over 35 languages.
- A growing number of U.S. companies are considering Incoterms® rules for domestic use.
- Incoterms® rules are self contained, right between the covers of Incoterms®2010.
- All Incoterms® rules have three-letter English language abbreviations.
- All Incoterms® rules must be accompanied by a geographic place, forcing the parties to consider what they are doing.
- Every Incoterms® rule is divided into 10 tasks in matching columns for quick reference. (Column A lists the seller's tasks and Column B lists the buyer's.) Besides providing handy checklists, this system guides the parties into additional contracts, such as transportation, that may be needed to complete the transaction. It also alerts the parties to possible regulatory compliance issues.
- Above all, Incoterms® rules reduce the potential for seller-buyer misunderstanding. This is the reason they exist.

CAVEATS

Besides noting the benefits that Incoterms® rules bring to contracts, users should be mindful of their limitations.

- As mentioned earlier, Incoterms® rules are not law and do not automatically apply unless specified in the sales contract. The preferred way of doing this is to write the abbreviation of the rule you are using and the accompanying place, followed by "Incoterms® 2010."
- Incoterms® rules do not indicate where title passes from the seller to the buyer. This important point should be addressed elsewhere in the sales contract.
- They do not address breach of contract issues. However, B5 and B6 of all Incoterms® 2010 rules provide for premature passage of risk and cost if the buyer fails to fulfill certain obligations.
- They are not all inclusive. Sellers and buyers must determine particular issues for themselves, such as how a given port or airport handles cargo in and out, what regulations a particular country imposes, etc.
- They exclude container loading from these rules in the definition of "packaging." Sellers and buyers should specify this task elsewhere in their contracts.
- They do not remove the need of the parties to specify an accompanying place, hopefully in as much detail as possible.
- "Drop shipments" can cause problems when the parties do not think things through. For instance, Party A (seller) sells goods to party B (buyer). Goods are manufactured by Party C, who may even be in a third country. The goods are to proceed directly from Party C to Party B. Which Incoterms rule applies? The answer is that there are really two contracts involved. Party A is the seller in its sales contract with Party B, but is the buyer in its purchase contract with Party C. Depending on the relationship between Party A and Party C, these two contracts may

or may not use the same Incoterms® rule. There's also the very practical concern that the correct documents should go to the correct party, which can require close monitoring.

- Stretching the FOB term: Americans accustomed to using the former Uniform Commercial Code shipment and delivery terms may be tempted to use the UCC FOB term for freight prepaid arrival contracts internationally and for all modes of transportation. This causes confusion as main carriage is never tasked to the seller in any of the F-Group Incoterms® rules. Further, the FOB Incoterms® rule is limited to use with waterborne main carriage. More in Chapter 19.
- Carriage obligation in FCA when accompanied by a location other than the seller's premises, FAS and FOB: A3 of FAS, FOB and FCA states that the seller has no obligation to contract for carriage. This means main carriage. In order to deliver, the seller is obligated to handle pre-carriage to get the goods to the place specified with FCA if other than its premises, or next to the vessel for FAS, or on the vessel for FOB.
- Exception to main carriage obligation in FAS, FOB and FCA: If the seller and buyer agree or if commercial practice and the buyer does not provide otherwise, this exception permits the seller to contract for main carriage at the buyer's risk and cost. I suggest this not be done except for special circumstances, and even then only when the seller and buyer expressly agree. The C-Group Incoterms® rules adequately address situations where the parties want the seller to contract for main carriage at the buyer's risk and cost without resorting to an exception. Merely arranging for main carriage without contracting for it is another thing entirely, and this should obviously be done at the buyer's risk and expense.
- The U.S. Government does not officially recognize Incoterms® rules, although some are mentioned in some regulations.
- For U.S. exports, there is an apparent conflict about export reporting between the Census Bureau's Foreign Trade Regulations and the F-Group Incoterms® rules. There is a way around this which we will address in Chapter 19.
- The use of D-Group Incoterms® rules may delay revenue recognition under accounting rules.
- Incoterms®2010 cannot address cargo security issues in any detail. The differences in country specific regulations are simply too great, and the frequency at which these change would make any detailed coverage immediately obsolete. The best we can do is to call the parties' attention to the fact that these regulations exist, and that a certain amount of information must be exchanged for compliance.
- The phrase "if customary" is used throughout Incoterms® 2010 but is nowhere defined.
- Variants to Incoterms® rules are possible. However, to the extent that the parties depart from the standard division of tasks they should explicitly state their intentions in their contracts. To minimize the use of variants, parties should check to see if another Incoterms® rule better matches their intentions.
- Incoterms® 2010 is written in a modern gender-neutral style. This reduces the possibility of using pronouns, and the reader may require a while to become accustomed to this.

[xiv] Incoterms® 2010, (ISBN 978-92-842-0080-1), ICC No. 720, ICC Publishing SA, Paris, France, available from ICC Publishing Inc., New York, NY
[xv] Incoterms 2000, (ISBN 92-842-1199-9), ICC No 560, ICC Publishing SA, Paris, France, available from ICC Publishing Inc., NY, NY

Chapter 5 - Offers and Proforma Invoices

Our last chapter described the role of shipment and delivery terms in purchase/sales contracts, which we'll continue calling "sales contracts." Depending on the nature of the goods and the size of the deal, these contracts can be anywhere from volumes of tightly written text to a simple exchange of promises. We'll leave the massive contracts to lawyers, and use the often quoted 80-20 rule which states that 20 percent of a company's customer base accounts for 80 percent of its business. This strongly implies numerous repeat sales, and frequently these are handled in an informal manner.

Reminder, I am not a lawyer. What you read is based on a considerable amount of commercial experience rather than legal training.

Bilateral contracts involve an exchange of promises. Someone makes an offer to another party. If that party agrees, it communicates its acceptance. Offers can be initiated by either party. Sellers can take the initiative by making offers to sell, commonly referred to as quotations. When buyers agree, they normally respond with purchase orders. Buyers can initiate issuing offers to purchase, sometimes as unsolicited purchase orders. Sellers can indicate their agreement by issuing acknowledgments, or in some cases by actually shipping.

Regardless of who starts the process, sales contracts result whenever offers and acceptances are in substantial agreement. There are entire bodies of law written about what "substantial agreement" means, and many companies employ self-serving boilerplate language on the forms they use. We aren't going there. There are also bodies of law about how offers are deemed to be delivered, how they can be withdrawn, etc., and we aren't going there either. Suffice to say that offers and corresponding acceptances do the job the vast majority of times.

As you will see in the next chapter, there are more "hoops and huddles" to clear in international trade than is true of domestic business. For this reason, international trade is also more structured and is more document intensive. After all, we are dealing with different countries with their particular regulations and often different languages. Savvy international sellers use documents called proforma invoices for their quotations. Since much of the information they contain should also be present in well conceived domestic quotations, readers primarily involved in domestic business should also find them interesting. Please also keep the minimum contract issues from Chapter Four in mind, as successful proforma invoices effectively become the seller's half of a sales contract.

PROFORMA INVOICES

These documents are often defined as "make believe invoices" and "sales quotations dressed up as invoices." Both are correct. Proforma invoices are sales quotations in invoice form. They are used primarily in international trade because:

- They recite all the details the seller thinks are important for the transaction.

- Regardless of language or custom, everyone in business recognizes an invoice for what it is.
- Governments also understand them, and this can be particularly important when buyers require import licenses or foreign exchange allocation.
- When sales contracts result, proformas become models for the commercial invoices which follow. This is particularly useful for parties using letter of credit payment terms, as proformas provide roadmaps for banks to use in issuing credits.
- When constructed to itemize cost increments, they enable buyers to determine whether they are better positioned to handle such tasks as freight and insurance. This would otherwise be difficult.
- They enable sellers to take the initiative by proposing the more seller-friendly Incoterms® rules (such as the C-Group).
- They make it easier for buyers to buy. Informed buyers want to know their total costs, not just merchandise prices.
- A correctly prepared proforma invoice indicates a level of experience on the seller's part. This can be very reassuring to buyers, particularly if no prior business relationship exists.

Important as these reasons are, the biggest benefit proforma invoices bring is that they force sellers to think their transactions through. This usually means consulting with other disciplines. Sales must provide the merchandise pricing and its validity period. Credit must indicate acceptable payment terms. Those "highly imaginative" people in charge of product availability must opine as to when the contract goods would be ready to ship in the event of an order. Speaking of time lines, buyers usually like to know when they can expect to receive the goods, particularly when sellers handle transportation. Obviously, both parties also need to determine who should handle transportation. This usually means sellers getting service availability and cost estimates from carriers and forwarders to offer buyers. Is insurance available, and at what cost?

Each proforma invoice should indicate the following information:

- the date the proforma invoice is prepared
- a unique proforma invoice number
- a reference to the buyer's inquiry, if any
- the seller's name and address
- the buyer's name and address
- any intermediate consignees, if known
- payment terms
- term of shipment and delivery (specific rule abbreviation + place + Incoterms® 2010) Note: the selected Incoterms® rule will indicate where the risk of loss passes from the seller to the buyer.
- a validity date to avoid an open ended commitment (usually a number of days from the proforma invoice date)
- an estimated shipment date (usually a number of days from the day an acceptable order is received)
- the currency of the transaction
- the body of law under which the offer is made and which will apply to any resulting contract
- the point where title passes from seller to buyer
- the quantity of the goods offered
- product description of the goods offered (perhaps including the six-digit HS number)
- unit price and total per line item

- total of all line items
- additional charges to conform to the cited Incoterms® rule. (Depending on the selected rule, these should include packaging and may also include where applicable: container loading, pre-carriage, forwarding, export clearance, heavy lift, out-port terminal handling, main carriage, conveyance unloading, destination port terminal handling, import clearance, on-carriage and insurance. We will cover these in the following chapter and again as we cover each Incoterms® rule individually.)
- a country of origin statement, if appropriate and important to the transaction
- any particular verbiage the customer's country may require if appropriate and if known.

The following proforma invoices are illustrative of the four groupings of Incoterms® rules: EXW, the F-Group, the C-Group and the D-Group. Under EXW, the seller bears no transportation responsibility at all and "delivers" when the shipment is available for pickup. With the exception of FCA accompanied by the seller's premises, F-Group sellers arrange and pay for pre-carriage. C-Group and D-Group sellers arrange and pay for pre-carriage and main carriage, and depending on the accompanying place, possibly on-carriage as well with CPT, CIP, DAP and DDP. (Keep in mind that we are referring <u>only</u> to arranging and paying for transportation with C-Group rules, as delivery happens when the goods are handed over to a carrier, not when they arrive at the accompanying place.)

We chose CIP as one of our illustrations as it speaks to insurance. Note our description of coverage as "London A clauses plus War and Strike, warehouse-to-warehouse," which exceeds the seller's minimum obligation. We also chose DAP along with the buyer's premises as it places most transport responsibility on the seller. Although the seller bears the risk of loss and is responsible for the condition of the goods until they arrive, there is no insurance obligation. Savvy sellers do insure, though, and many either bury the premium cost in their merchandise price or charge the buyer for it as a separate line item. We chose the latter in our example as some countries assess duty only on the value of the goods themselves. Note that the CIP and DAP proforma totals are the same as they include identical cost increments. Only the point of delivery differs (first carrier with CIP, buyer's premises with DAP).

Done correctly, proforma invoices show the buyer what the seller is prepared to do and at what price. By itemizing the cost increments, the strengths and weaknesses in delivered pricing can be pinpointed. When done consistently, they provide a database which makes subsequent proformas easier to prepare. Above all, they help avoid misunderstandings, thus making sellers and buyers more comfortable in dealing with each other.

Our proformas show items like governing law and dispute resolution right on the front as there is no back. In practice, these are often recited on the back of the document along with other boilerplate language.

PROFORMA INVOICE

EXPORTER International Projects, Inc. 1150 South McCord Road Holland, OH 43528 USA	**PROFORMA INVOICE #** 5.1	**PROFORMA INVOICE DATE** September 20, 2010	
	PROFORMA VALIDITY DATE October 20, 2010	**EST'D SHIPMENT DATE** September 30, 2010	
SOLD TO Callahan & Riddle Ltd. Maple Grove Plains London E2E Q94 ENGLAND	**TERMS OF PAYMENT** Net 30 days		
	SHIPMENT/DELIVERY TERMS EXW 1150 South McCord Road, Holland, OH 43528 USA, Incoterms 2010		
SHIP TO Pick Up	**TITLE** Ownership transfers when payment is received by seller		

QUANTITY	UNITS	DESCRIPTION OF MERCHANDISE	UNIT PRICE	TOTAL
300	Each	How to Better Your Golf Game – HS 950490	5.00	1500.00

LAW & DISPUTE RESOLUTION: The U.N. Convention on Contracts for the International Sale of Goods (1980) shall apply to this offer and any resulting contract. Any disputes will be resolved by binding arbitration services of the International Chamber of Commerce.	**MERCHANDISE TOTAL** Export Packing	**US$** 1500.00 75.00
	GRAND TOTAL EXW Holland, Ohio	**US$** 1575.00

PROFORMA INVOICE

EXPORTER International Projects, Inc. 1150 South McCord Road Holland, OH 43528 USA	**PROFORMA INVOICE #** 5.2
	PROFORMA INVOICE DATE September 21, 2010
	PROFORMA VALIDITY DATE October 21, 2010
	EST'D SHIPMENT DATE September 30, 2010
SOLD TO Callahan & Riddle Ltd. Maple Grove Plains London E2E Q94 ENGLAND	**TERMS OF PAYMENT** Net 30 days
	SHIPMENT/DELIVERY TERMS FCA Air America Terminal 2, Columbus Airport, Columbus, OH, USA, Incoterms 2010
SHIP TO Air America Terminal 2 Columbus Airport Columbus, Ohio, USA	**TITLE** Ownership transfers when payment is received by seller

QUANTITY	UNITS	DESCRIPTION OF MERCHANDISE	UNIT PRICE	TOTAL
300	Each	How to Better Your Golf Game – HS 950490	5.00	1500.00

LAW & DISPUTE RESOLUTION: The U.N. Convention on Contracts for the International Sale of Goods (1980) shall apply to this offer and any resulting contract. Any disputes will be resolved by binding arbitration services of the International Chamber of Commerce.	**MERCHANDISE TOTAL** Export Packing Pre-carriage	**US$** 1500.00 75.00 30.00
	GRAND TOTAL FCA Columbus Airport	**US$** 1605.00

PROFORMA INVOICE

EXPORTER International Projects, Inc. 1150 South McCord Road	**PROFORMA INVOICE #** 5.3 **PROFORMA INVOICE DATE** September 22, 2010 **PROFORMA VALIDITY DATE** October 22, 2010 **EST'D SHIPMENT DATE** September 30, 2010
SOLD TO Callahan & Riddle Ltd. Maple Grove Plains London E2E Q94 ENGLAND	**TERMS OF PAYMENT** Net 30 days **SHIPMENT/DELIVERY TERMS** CIP Maple Grove Plains, London, England, Incoterms 2010
SHIP TO Same as SOLD TO	**TITLE** Ownership transfers when payment is received by seller

QUANTITY	UNITS	DESCRIPTION OF MERCHANDISE	UNIT PRICE	TOTAL
300	Each	How to Better Your Golf Game – HS 950490	5.00	1500.00

LAW & DISPUTE RESOLUTION: The U.N. Convention on Contracts for the International Sale of Goods (1980) shall apply to this offer and any resulting contract. Any disputes will be resolved by binding arbitration services of the International Chamber of Commerce.

MERCHANDISE TOTAL	**US$** 1500.00
Export Packing	75.00
Pre-carriage	30.00
Main carriage and on-carriage	190.00
Insurance (A+ War & Strike) (warehouse to warehouse)	23.07
GRAND TOTAL CIP Maple Grove Plains	**US$** 1818.07

PROFORMA INVOICE

EXPORTER International Projects, Inc. 1150 South McCord Road Holland, OH 43528 USA	**PROFORMA INVOICE #** 5.4 **PROFORMA INVOICE DATE** September 23, 2010 **PROFORMA VALIDITY DATE** October 23, 2010 **EST'D SHIPMENT DATE** September 30, 2010
SOLD TO Callahan & Riddle Ltd. Maple Grove Plains London E2E Q94 ENGLAND	**TERMS OF PAYMENT** Net 30 days **SHIPMENT/DELIVERY TERMS** DAP Maple Grove Plains, London, England, Incoterms 2010
SHIP TO Same as SOLD TO	**TITLE** Ownership transfers when payment is received by seller

QUANTITY	UNITS	DESCRIPTION OF MERCHANDISE	UNIT PRICE	TOTAL
300	Each	How to Better Your Golf Game – HS 950490	5.00	1500.00

LAW & DISPUTE RESOLUTION: The U.N. Convention on Contracts for the International Sale of Goods (1980) shall apply to this offer and any resulting contract. Any disputes will be resolved by binding arbitration services of the International Chamber of Commerce.	**MERCHANDISE TOTAL** Export Packing Pre-carriage Main carriage and on-carriage Insurance (A+ War & Strike) (warehouse to warehouse)	**US$** 1500.00 75.00 30.00 190.00 23.07
	GRAND TOTAL DAP Maple Grove Plains	**US$** 1818.07

Chapter 6 - Hoops, Hurdles and Contracts

HOOPS AND HURDLES

Hoops and hurdles are what I call the things that must happen for a shipment to get from the seller to the buyer. We'll look at them first and then consider the contracts used to navigate them. Readers interested in international trade will get much more out of the first part of this chapter than will those interested in using Incoterms® rules for domestic business only. Still, it's worth reading for domestic-only folk, if for no other reason than at least one leg of an international shipment normally involves domestic transportation.

Whenever I do a live seminar on Incoterms® rules, I proclaim one side of the room to be the seller's country and the other the buyer's. I then begin to walk across the room, starting from the "seller's premises" (which is represented by the wall on the "seller's side") and going toward the buyer's, ending with the "buyer's premises" (represented by the opposite wall). As I move along, I stop at the departure point from the seller's side, about ¼ of the way. This represents a seaport or an airport, and the walk to it simulates pre-carriage. I then simulate main carriage by proceeding to a point about ¾ of the way. This brings me to the arrival point on the buyer's side. I then finish walking to the far wall to simulate on-carriage to the buyer's premises.

My stroll is usually rewarded by a "now I've got it" look from many attendees. All the hoops and hurdles I describe along the way exist at least to some extent in all international shipments and to a lesser extent in domestic transactions. So, as good sportscasters say when broadcasting a football game on the radio: "moving from left to right on your dial."

INTERNATIONAL SHIPMENTS

<u>At the seller's premises</u>

- Someone must provide the goods. This is the seller. There's more, though. The goods should be the correct goods and they should be provided when promised. (Make sure those highly imaginative people in charge of product availability read this – many companies have at least one.)
- Someone must suitably package the goods. The introduction to <u>Incoterms®2010</u>[xvi] specifies that this must be as mentioned in the sales contract and suitable for transport. It specifically excludes container loading, with the recommendation that this task be addressed elsewhere in the sales contract. I have another caveat about "suitable for transport." If the seller is not involved in main carriage (as with EXW and FCA), and would not otherwise know how it is to take place, the buyer should provide any required packing information before the contract is

concluded. Different transport modes require different degrees of packing, the most heroic being for non-containerized shipments by vessel. Buyers should agree to pay for reasonable packaging costs as receiving undamaged shipments is very much in their interest.

- Someone must load the collecting conveyance, and for all but EXW this is a seller obligation.
- Someone must arrange and pay for pre-carriage. This could be either the seller or the buyer, depending on the rule selected and its accompanying place.

<u>At the departure point on the seller's side (a port, airport or possibly a border location)</u>

- Someone should arrange for the goods to be received by the main carrier, and this would usually be the party handling main carriage transportation. For FCA, the seller is not responsible for unloading the pre-carriage delivering vehicle, as the buyer-appointed carrier or forwarder would probably have the people and equipment to do so.
- Someone must arrange for and pay for main carriage. This may be either the buyer (EXW or F-Group Rules) or the seller (C-Group and D-Group Rules).
- Before the shipment can leave the seller's country, someone must arrange and pay for export clearance. The U.S. does not impose export duty but some countries do, so importers beware. All Incoterms® rules except EXW make the seller responsible for export clearance, as it seems most logical to have people deal with their own governments whenever possible. However, for U.S. exports, the Census Bureau Foreign Trade Regulations dictate that if the forwarder is appointed by the buyer, as is usually the case with EXW and F-Group rules, the forwarder should report the export. There is a remedy for this which we will explain in Chapter 19. Besides the mere reporting of U.S. exports, a determination must be made about whether a license is required and, if not, why not. For some items, the licensing process can be time consuming and with no guarantee of success. Savvy sellers of such items do their homework before executing a sales contract. Further, there are "bad guy" lists which over the years have been growing both in number and length. Trade with such people, companies and countries is prohibited or severely restricted. (The good news is that as of this writing (2010), significant reforms are promised to simplify U.S. export control. This would be an excellent step towards increasing U.S. exports.)
- Someone must load the main carrier. Main carriers who follow shipping schedules normally load their own ships and planes. Since they call on the same ports/airports, they have arrangements in place for this. However, non-scheduled carriers such as "tramp vessels" have no such fixed rotation, and may not be able or willing to load. The FOB Incoterms® rule accommodates this for waterborne shipments by holding the seller responsible for loading despite the fact that the contract of main carriage is between the buyer and the carrier. This makes it useful for vessel chartering, but inappropriate for containerized shipments with ship lines that load their own vessels.

<u>At the arrival point on the buyer's side</u>

- Someone must unload the carrier. This brings in a potentially contentious issue, particularly for vessel transport. There is no set worldwide policy among carriers about who pays unloading and related terminal handling charges. Many contracts of carriage do not include unloading and other "destination charges" while some do. It may depend on the destination, in which currency the carrier wants payment, and local regulations. It may also depend on the bargaining power of the party negotiating transportation with the carrier, and who knows what else. A problem occurs when the seller pays unloading and other destination charges as part of the carriage contract and the buyer is also charged for them. The buyer could wind up paying for these twice: once to the seller as part of the freight component of the selling price, and again to the carrier. Incoterms®2010 addresses this as best it can in the CPT, CIP, CFR, CIF, DAT, DAP and DDP rules by cautioning the parties to clearly specify in their sales contracts the point to which carriage is to be paid. It then warns sellers to contract for carriage to this point because buyers are not required to reimburse sellers for charges paid for carriage beyond it.

- Someone must arrange import clearance. The logic of having people deal with their own countries continues here. All rules except DDP task the buyer with import clearance. Under DDP, the seller is responsible for import clearance and all import taxes including VAT. This seems odd to me, as buyers in countries with VAT would probably be better placed to get any permissible refunds than would foreign sellers. However, I am not a VAT expert, there's no U.S. VAT, and the DDP Guidance Note indicates that the parties may agree otherwise.
- Someone must arrange for on-carriage. Again, this could be the seller or the buyer, depending on the agreed Incoterms® rule and the designated place.

At the buyer's premises

- Someone must unload the delivering vehicle. The only rule that tasks the seller with unloading is DAT, which is designed for use with a terminal, quay or container yard rather than with a buyer's premises. Again, the default follows logic as the buyer would probably be better positioned to unload at its own premises than would the remote seller. The parties can always agree otherwise in their sales contract if they really want to.
- While Incoterms® rules do not address this issue, common sense dictates that someone at the buyer's premises examine the condition of the incoming goods and claim on carriers and/or insurers as necessary. This nicely segues into the next topic.

How about insurance?

This should obviously be addressed while the sales contract is being negotiated. While all Incoterms® 2010 rules address risk of loss transfer, only two obligate anyone to insure. CIP and CIF task the seller with providing insurance, but the minimum coverage specified in the default position is very limited and should probably be enhanced.

A number of ICC National Committees suggested that the default position be reversed to require sellers to provide "maximum" cover, called Institute Cargo Clauses A or "All Risks." However, insurers were polled and recommended that this not be done. Typical perils differ by product type, and the type of coverage needed varies accordingly from industry to industry and even from one insured to another. This would make it difficult to define what "maximum coverage" would be for any given situation. Minimum coverage is much easier to define. There's also the practical reason that because of its low cost, minimum cover offers a solution where a party is required to purchase insurance from local and often substandard insurers.

Both CIP and CIF specify the default amount of insurance at 110% of the CIP or CIF value, and that it be in the currency of the contract. It must continue until the goods have reached at least the named destination place.

For the other Incoterms® rules, the parties need to consider their own risk positions in the transaction and agree on insurance coverage outside of the rule. For EXW and FCA + origin point, the seller bears no transport risk. For FCA + another place on the seller's side and FAS, the seller is at risk for pre-carriage. FOB has pre-carriage risk plus the risk to the goods during vessel loading.

(Note: Many insurers offer "FAS/FOB coverage for this.) In CPT, the buyer bears the risk from the "first carrier" and should consider "warehouse to warehouse" coverage. Under CFR, the seller remains at risk through vessel loading. Buyers using the CIF or CIP rules may consider purchasing "contingency insurance" which is insurance coverage against default by the seller's insurer. D-Group rules are used in arrival contracts where the seller remains responsible for the condition of the goods up to the agreed place. Savvy sellers insure accordingly.

During the revision, the ICC National Committees of several countries supported the idea of providing a new F-Group Incoterms® rule requiring the seller to insure. A number of insurers polled about this indicated that it would not work well. Since under these rules some or all transportation is done by the buyers, sellers would not be able to take steps to reduce transport risk. In fact, under the FCA rule, sellers may not even know the identity of the main carriers, and their insurers would be "blindly" providing coverage.

There may be more involved than merely risk for the condition of the goods, which passes at "delivery" per A5-B5 of all Incoterms® rules. Regardless of where loss or damage occurs, a buyer who prepays may want some assurance other than the possibility of hauling the seller into court. There are also such issues as security interests, retentions of title, liens, etc. which may well address post-delivery events. Insurance products exist to cover these, but we're getting beyond the scope of this book.

DOMESTIC SHIPMENTS

These start the same way international shipments do, with the seller providing the correct goods, appropriately packaged and loaded on the collecting vehicle. Fortunately, there are fewer hoops and hurdles involved for most domestic shipments. A single carrier frequently provides door-to-door service. However, for large shipping pieces and commodities, there may be transshipments involving several different carriers in different modes with individual contracts of carriage. Think of moving a heavy turbine by rail, barge and finally by truck. Even air freight shipments may be handled on an airport-to-airport basis, picked up and delivered at either end by local carriers independent of the airline, or by sellers and buyers themselves.

There is no export or import clearance for purely domestic transactions. However, sellers should make sure they are involved in purely domestic transactions rather than acting as U.S. Principal Parties in Interest for exports. For instance, if you receive an order from a U.S. company, and that company will export the goods, you have a domestic transaction as far as export reporting is concerned. (You should still watch out for "red flags" that would indicate an unauthorized export, and it's always a good idea to insist on knowing the destination country for many reasons.) On the other hand, if you receive an order from a foreign buyer, with instructions to deliver to a forwarder here, you probably are the USPPI. We will cover this further in Chapter 19.

In-transit damage can happen to domestic shipments, and someone should insure them. Often, these are covered by inland-marine provisions of blanket policies. See the insurance contracts section below.

CONTRACTS

Now that we've seen what needs to occur, let's look at the contracts that make them happen.

Contracts of carriage

Carriage contracts are evidenced by transport documents. These outline the terms of carriage between the carrier and the person contracting with it. (Actually, most don't go into much detail, but instead refer to a remote master contract terms and conditions that few people bother to read.) At a minimum, they should indicate the party contracting with the carrier, a description of the goods being shipped, whether the freight cost is prepaid or collect, any additional non-freight carrier charges and services, and to whom the shipment should be released on arrival. Some carriers also provide COD service for the value of the goods.

We Americans tend to use the term "shipper" loosely to mean the party providing the goods for transport. Normally, this is the seller. Strictly speaking, this is true only when the seller contracts for carriage. Sellers who ship freight collect and do not contract for carriage are really "consignors" rather than shippers. Since in these situations the buyer contracts for carriage, the buyer is really the shipper. Most people at this time (mid 2010) bow to convention and refer to freight-collect sellers as shippers. However, when the Rotterdam Rules[xvii] come into force, there will be clear distinctions at least for vessel shipments.

Sellers using F-Group Incoterms® rules should make sure they have a right to the transport document if this is important to them. This is particularly important for payment terms such as documentary letters of credit and documentary collections where one of the documents required for payment purposes is a correctly executed transport document. Don't forget, under these terms the contract of main carriage is between the carrier and the buyer, not the seller. The forwarder is most likely also working for the buyer. The seller has no control over the transport document, and may not even be able to obtain it.

Marine transportation documents come in several versions, and the differences can be important to both sellers and buyers.

- Negotiable (also called "order") bills of lading contain the word ORDER in the consignee field and are bearer instruments. They are often issued in multiple copies, and carriers will not release such shipments unless at least one original document is surrendered. Negotiable bills of lading serve two different purposes. They permit the sale of goods in transit by simply endorsing and passing the originals to subsequent buyers. Sellers can also use them to enforce documentary collection payment terms by sending them to a bank in the buyer's country with instructions not to release them until the buyer pays or accepts a draft (a promise to pay).
- Non-negotiable marine transport documents (often called non-negotiable bills of lading or sea waybills) do not contain the word ORDER in the consignee field. Instead, a party's name appears, usually the buyer. These are not bearer documents, and the carrier may or may not insist on their surrender depending on its own policy. Paperless marine transport documents (sometimes called data freight releases) also fall under this category.
- "On-board" marine transportation documents indicate that the goods have actually been loaded on the vessel, and show an on-board date. These may be either negotiable or non-

negotiable. They are appropriate to FOB, CFR and CIF, since these Incoterms® rules task the seller with vessel loading.

- Received-for-shipment marine transport documents indicate that the carrier has received the goods for shipment on the intended vessel but without indicating that they have been loaded on board. These are appropriate for FCA, CPT and CIP, and with a stretch to FAS as well.

Air waybills normally do not bear on-board notations as air cargo usually moves soon after the carrier receives it. They are never negotiable (along with all other transport documents ending with "waybill").

We North Americans call the document covering truck shipments a "bill of lading," but it is called a "CMR" (International Road Transportation Convention) document in Europe and countries that follow European practices. As drivers do not sign until loading is completed, truck bills of lading are "on board." I am told that a negotiable truck bill of lading is possible, but have never seen one and can't imagine how it would play out with a truck line.

Rail waybills are usually on board and are non-negotiable (that "waybill" word).

Integrated small package service transport documents are usually paperless unless the package is brought to the carrier's facility. They, too, are non-negotiable.

<u>Insurance contracts</u>
Insurance can be purchased in several ways and from several parties (insurers, forwarders and carriers).

"Marine cargo" insurance covers vessel shipments and may also be used for air shipments. It may be purchased on a per-shipment basis from an insurer, and the resulting document is called a policy. It also may be bought against a master cargo policy, and the policy owner would issue an insurance certificate describing the terms of coverage for each covered shipment. Larger shippers have their own master cargo policies. Smaller shippers may buy insurance against someone else's master cargo policy (usually a forwarder's), and the policy owner would issue a certificate for each covered shipment.

Marine cargo insurance coverage can be transferred (usually from seller to buyer) by showing the transferees name as the assured. Insurance certificates can also be written in negotiable form.

Some carriers offer insurance on shipments they transport. This may be expressed as an insurance premium or an additional valuation charge increasing the carrier's liability. Either of these would show up on the paper or electronic transport document.

The most important thing to remember about marine cargo insurance is that premiums are generally payable per use. While some large policy owners and their insurers may agree on an average overall single premium, the underlying calculations are based on use. With this possible exception, insurance coverage is not automatic, and the insurer must be notified of each covered shipment. One cannot simply assume that a given shipment is covered by marine cargo insurance unless the policy owner reports it to the insurer.

"Inland marine" is the insurance that covers domestic shipments. The name comes from the fact that it was initially developed by underwriters from the older marine cargo insurance industry. Unlike marine cargo insurance, inland marine is usually purchased for a flat premium per covered time period, and automatically attaches to the policy owner's outward domestic shipments. However, inland marine insurance usually does not cover international shipments.

It is normally the policy owner who makes a claim with inland marine coverage. Some tweaking is needed when using either CIP or CIF domestically, as these rules specify that the insurance must enable the buyer or anyone with insurable interest to claim directly on the insurer. A simple written promise from the seller that it will make any needed insurance claims on behalf of the buyer should solve this.

Payment Contracts

International sales contracts sometimes stipulate that payment will be made by letter of credit (L/C). There are two basic types, standby and documentary.

- A standby credit pays when something doesn't happen, for instance, when a payment it guarantees wasn't made or a contract it guarantees wasn't completed. Since it is impossible to prove a negative, these normally require mere certifications by the beneficiary that the covered event did not take place and that payment is due.
- A documentary credit pays when something happens, and in the case of sales contract that "something" is normally a shipment. Events can be proven by documents, and as their name implies documentary credits will require the presentation of documents to trigger payments. Banks strictly apply the terms and conditions of a letter of credit, along with the governing letter of credit rules (UCP 600 as of this writing) and a broader set of procedures called International Standard Banking Practice (ISBP).[xviii] When sellers are L/C beneficiaries, it is important that they check the documentary requirements against the sales contract to make sure they agree. Obviously, they should also make sure they are capable of providing the required documents within any timelines specified in the L/C.

[xvi] Incoterms® 2010, (ISBN 978-92-842-0080-1), ICC No. 720, ICC Publishing SA, Paris, France, available from ICC Publishing Inc., New York, NY

[xvii] United Nations Convention on Contracts for the International Carriage of Goods by Sea, was signed in Rotterdam September 2009, and as of this writing (summer 2010) is awaiting ratification by at least 20 countries to come into force.

[xviii] Both are available from ICC Publishing Inc., NY, NY

PART III – COMMENTARY ON INDIVIDUAL INCOTERMS® 2010 RULES

Chapter 7 - Introduction to Part III – Story Line

Now that we've done our background work, it's time to cover the eleven Incoterms® 2010 rules themselves. This introduction will explain our approach and provide some orientation.

We'll assume that you already have a copy of the official Incoterms® 2010[xix], and suggest that you keep it handy. This revision includes guidance notes, which greatly simplify my job of explaining how each rule works in practice. I'll summarize the parties' responsibilities. Also, I will call your attention to points I think may appear odd at first, and explain them in everyday business English. Important changes from previous Incoterms® versions will be stressed. Payment term implications for international transactions will also be mentioned.

Sometimes, it's easier to narrate than to simply present bare facts. This seemed to work well in the past, so we'll continue following a story line. Those of you have kindly read previous versions of Incoterms for Americans® will recognize some characters we've used to demonstrate how Incoterms® rules are used in (almost) real life situations.

Otto III is the third generation German buyer. Like his father and grandfather before him, he is a widget importer, speaks no English, and has never visited the United States. His warehouse is located in Baden Baden, an inland German location. The company has been doing so well that the entire older generation has retired and moved to Tahiti, leaving poor Otto to run the company on a "learn by doing" basis. Since Otto III sounds more like a Holy Roman Emperor than a widget importer, we'll simply call him Otto.

Glotz Industries manufactures widgets at Fort Wayne, Indiana, an inland U.S. location. Years ago, its sales manager located Otto's grandfather as a potential customer. An excellent relationship developed, and Otto's company became one of Glotz's largest accounts. The sales manager retired, and all shipping records were lost in a flood. No one at Glotz speaks German, or knows anything about Baden Baden other than that's where they had been shipping all those widgets.

We'll simplify the story by specifying that widgets are controlled by the Commerce Department's Bureau of Industry and Security (BIS) and are correctly classified as EAR99. Glotz's export control responsibilities are therefore largely limited to avoiding the bad guys, bad places and bad uses found in various government lists, and to accurate Electronic Export Information (EEI) filing for reportable export shipments.

The idea of Otto and Glotz being able to do business with each other over the language barrier seems like a recipe for disaster. However, they can communicate at least basic contract related information by using Incoterms® 2010 which is available in both English and German. They both understand and recognize proforma invoices and purchase orders. They have also purchased a basic sales contract abstract[xx] from the ICC, and use that as a template for structuring their translations. Above all, they trust each other, thanks to the long-standing relationship the two companies enjoy.

Andre is a French widget manufacturer located in Strasbourg, about 30 minutes by train from Baden Baden. He had been supplying Otto for years, but lost a substantial amount of business to Glotz. The fact that Germany and France are both Euro zone members alternatively helps and hurts Andre's chances, depending on the U.S. dollar exchange rate.

Gordie Lefevre is a Canadian widget importing distributor located in North Bay, Ontario. He began importing Glotz's widgets soon after they became duty free under the NAFTA. As he buys on net-30 day payment terms, there's no concern about documents except for the NAFTA origin certificate which Glotz provides once a year on a blanket basis.

Mexican battery manufacturer Gerardo Jesus Prieto de la Torre (Jerry) uses Glotz's widgets as a component at his Monterrey factory. Like Gordie, he buys on open account payment terms and requires a NAFTA certificate of origin. Since the Mexican import clearance process is more demanding than in Canada, Jerry uses a freight forwarder-customs broker with offices in Laredo, Texas and Nuevo Laredo, Mexico.

Riddle Enterprises is a Seattle distributor which has been handling Glotz's widgets for many years. Business is done on open account payment terms. Riddle normally places large orders for freight savings, but sometimes needs next-day delivery to supply an urgent customer requirement.

Illustrations can help to bring concepts home, and you have undoubtedly noticed that Incoterms® 2010 provides them. We can also illustrate through comparison to familiar situations and documents. Proforma invoices suit this purpose very well, and we will see them as part of our story line for each Incoterms® rule.

[xix] Incoterms®2010 (ISBN 978-92-842-0080-1), ICC No. 720, ICC Publishing SA, Paris, France, available from ICC Publishing Inc., New York, NY

[xx] ICC Model International Sales Contract (ISBN 978-92-842-1210-1), ICC No. 556, ICC Publishing SA, Paris, France, available from ICC Publishing Inc., New York, NY

Chapter 8 - Ex Works

Abbreviation: EXW
Transport mode: all (or more precisely, none)
Contract type: shipment
Place: where the shipment begins (usually the seller's premises)

Ex Works (EXW) is the Incoterms® rule with minimum seller responsibility. All the seller needs to do is have the goods suitably packaged at the stipulated place and at the agreed time, and promptly notify the buyer that they are ready. The seller merely supplies the goods without any transportation arrangements, so it falls to the buyer to arrange them. Further, the seller is not responsible for loading the collecting conveyance, and delivers once the goods have been made available. Finally, under <u>only</u> this Incoterms® rule, the seller has no export clearance obligation. (See the American Viewpoint section of this chapter for the reason this doesn't work well for us.)

Since the seller undertakes no transportation responsibility, the stipulated place is usually the seller's own premises. This should be described in geographic terms in as much detail as possible, including addresses, such as EXW 1150 South McCord Rd., Holland, Ohio, Incoterms® 2010.

EXW may be used with all means of transport. For this reason, the seller's obligation to suitably package may largely depend upon the buyer making the seller aware of the transportation arrangements, particularly for exports. For instance, if the buyer gives the seller reason to believe that shipment will be made by air, and changes plans without the seller's knowledge, the seller would not know to provide the robust packaging required for ocean shipments. **Also, the packaging definition found in <u>Incoterms® 2010</u>[xxi] states that these rules do not cover container stowage and that this should be covered elsewhere in the sales contract. This is new.**

At first, EXW seems attractive, particularly for sellers who wish to avoid getting involved with shipping and export control. All the seller need do is have the product ready to ship when agreed, put it in a suitable box, get it to the loading dock, and notify the buyer. However, a quick visit to the American Viewpoint section of this chapter will reveal the downsides.

EXW is so one-sided that buyers have difficulty with it. In fact, I had to really use my imagination to come up with a suitable export scenario. There is a common use in domestic business, though, with small package carriers whose drivers typically load their trucks.

BUYER-SELLER RESPONSIBILITIES

The following is a short list of responsibilities.

1. **Goods and Payment**
   The seller must have the goods available when promised, suitably packaged, and must notify the buyer that they are available for pickup. The buyer must pay the seller.
   EXW may be used with all means of transport. For this reason, the seller's obligation to suitably package may largely depend upon the buyer making the seller aware of the transportation arrangements, particularly for export transactions. For instance, if the buyer gives the seller reason to believe that shipment will be made by air, and changes plans without the seller's knowledge, the seller would not know to provide the robust packaging required for ocean shipments. **Also, the packaging definition found in Incoterms® 2010[xxii] states that these rules do not cover container stowage and that this should be covered elsewhere in the sales contract. This is new.**
2. **Loading the collecting conveyance**
   The seller has no responsibility to load. Common practice is that the seller does load, and most willingly exceed their responsibility under this rule. However, this can open the door for controversy in case of damage during loading. This term works best for shipments with carriers that typically load their own conveyances.
3. **Pre-carriage**
   The seller is not responsible. This presents no particular problem with domestic shipments. No particular problem for international shipments either if buyer has "door-to-somewhere" carriage contracts. When this isn't the case, foreign buyers could be put in an awkward situation of trying to arrange pre-carriage in the seller's country.
4. **Export clearance**
   This is a buyer responsibility under this rule. Regardless, U.S. export regulations bring the seller into the picture as the United States Principal Party in Interest (USPPI). See the American Viewpoint section of this chapter. U.S. importers could also face problems complying with the export control regulations of their suppliers' countries. Some countries charge export duty.
5. **Other hoops and hurdles**
   The parties must work together on cargo security information. This usually means one party telling the other what is required and the other party providing it. Since security regulations change often and vary from country to country and from one transport mode to another, Incoterms® rules are limited to making the parties aware that they must be addressed. For EXW this is covered in A2 and A10-B10.
6. **Insurance**
   Neither party is required to insure under EXW. However, common sense dictates otherwise, and insurance should be addressed outside of the rule. This is particularly important for buyers because risk of loss passes from the seller to the buyer when the seller delivers, which happens prior to any transportation.
7. **Documentary implications**
   a. Commercial Documents: The seller should provide a commercial invoice, a packing list, and any other commercial documents cited in the sales contract.
   b. Transport Documents: The seller is not required to provide a transport document as the buyer is contracting for all transportation. In fact, under B8, the buyer must provide the seller with proof of having taken delivery. (An exception would be a freight collect pre-carriage bill of lading where the seller exceeds its obligation by loading the collecting conveyance or with a carrier that handles loading.)
   c. Export Control Documentation: The seller has no obligation to the buyer for export clearance. However, as the USPPI, the seller is obligated to provide company and product specific information to the buyer-appointed agent for EEI filing. With the possible exception

of specific export licenses, there is no longer a paper document involved as U.S. export reporting is done electronically.

d. Import Entry Documentation: This is a buyer obligation. However, A10 requires the seller to provide assistance at the buyer's request, risk and cost.

8. **Payment terms considerations**

   By definition, the buyer must arrange for pick-up at the stipulated place under the EXW Incoterms® rule. It then follows that the seller must be prepared to turn the goods over at that place. Since there's no way to use documents to restrict possession of the goods, the credit decision becomes either total trust or no trust at all.

STORY LINE

Otto and Andre

Otto is a young importer of widgets located in Baden Baden, Germany. Andre is Otto's French widget supplier, located in Strasbourg, France, quite near the German border. Otto buys from Andre using the EXW Incoterms® rule as shown in Andre's proforma invoice 8.1. He simply drives his truck to Andre's premises, loads, and returns home to Baden Baden, usually in time for lunch. Pre-carriage, main carriage and on-carriage are all handled by Otto in his truck. There is no export clearance or import clearance formalities between France and Germany as both are EU members.

Otto and Glotz

As we saw in Chapter 7, Otto wishes to purchase from Glotz Industries, a Fort Wayne widget manufacturer. Although the parties have enjoyed a longstanding relationship, neither has access to the way business had been conducted in the past. Both are literally starting from scratch.

As shown in proforma invoice 8.2, Glotz proposed the EXW Incoterms® rule in their first price quotation to Otto. The idea of making transportation arrangements from a factory in an unknown part of a foreign country – in compliance with unknown export control and cargo security procedures – was more than Otto was prepared to handle. He requested Glotz to assume more of the transaction burden by quoting under a different Incoterms® rule. We'll see the results in subsequent chapters.

Gordie and Glotz

Canadian importing distributor Gordie has been buying Glotz widgets for many years. He is also a race car enthusiast, and has attended the Indy 500 every year since 1972. Since each trip takes him past Glotz's Fort Wayne factory, he mixes business with pleasure by driving down in his truck and picking up a load of widgets on his way home. These sales are handled on an EXW basis. Shipments of widgets to Canada do not require export licenses, so there's no required export reporting. All Gordie needs is a commercial invoice and a copy of the blanket NAFTA certificate of origin. He even loads the truck himself, as he usually picks up the weekend following the race when Glotz's loading crew is not at work.

Proforma invoice 8.3 is typical of what Gordie gets from Glotz before leaving Canada. It is similar to the kind Andre sends Otto, since both parties handle transportation, are willing to load their own trucks, and face no export clearance hurdles.

Riddle and Glotz

Riddle distributes Glotz's widgets throughout the Pacific Northwest. They usually purchase in truckload quantities, but occasionally require next day delivery to meet a customer's urgent requirements. Glotz normally provides proforma invoices as order acknowledgments to their large distributors to inform them when a shipment is leaving and what it contains and therefore help them balance their inventories. This procedure is followed even for small shipments.

Riddle has negotiated some excellent next-day delivery freight rates with a small package carrier. They always place urgently needed orders on an EXW basis, since they are arranging and paying for all transportation and unlike larger shipments the driver loads his own truck. See Glotz's proforma invoice 8.4.

AMERICAN VIEWPOINT

International use

For reasons that are very obvious to Otto and any other foreign buyer, few U.S. export sales contracts are concluded on the EXW Incoterms® rule. Even buyers that have arranged "door-to-door" transportation and have forwarders willing to handle the export clearance obligation would encounter the problem of loading the collecting conveyance.

The United States has a policy whereby all exports are subject to some degree of control. Although other federal government agencies have some jurisdiction, the lion's share of export control is managed by the United States Department of Commerce, Bureau of Industry & Security (BIS). For most items, it determines whether a shipment of a given product to a given party in a given country for a given end use may be shipped without a license or under a license exception. If an export license is required, it must be secured from BIS or other federal agency having jurisdiction before shipment can legally take place. Other federal agencies with significant export control jurisdiction include the Department of the Treasury, Office of Foreign Assets Control (OFAC) and the State Department Directorate of Defense Trade Controls (DDTC). They and BIS maintain separate "bad guy" lists of parties and countries to which trade is restricted. Without some pretty sophisticated U.S. representation, foreign buyers would find it almost impossible to understand and comply with all these export regulations.

Until the Census Bureau's Foreign Trade Statistical Regulations (FTSR) was revised in early 2000s some U.S. exporters tried to use EXW to distance themselves from any export control compliance responsibility. The FTSR and subsequent Foreign Trade Regulations of 2008 prevent this by introducing the concept of U.S. Principal Party in Interest (USPPI), which includes EXW sellers. See Chapter 19 for more information on export reporting.

Sometimes, a foreign buyer will ask a U.S. exporter to go beyond its EXW responsibility and handle export clearance. This can be risky for the exporter, as under EXW the seller has no control or even firsthand knowledge of any transportation. (Think of a buyer leaving the seller's loading dock in a taxi.) This could open the door for all manner of illegal diversion.

The EXW Incoterms® rule can also facilitate export diversion that does not violate regulations but may disrupt the seller's export distribution. Let's say a seller has cultivated a relationship with an excellent French importing distributor. This distributor is a textbook case of doing it right: places large orders frequently, never runs out of stock, pays correctly, aggressively promotes the line and provides excellent after-sale service. These efforts result in that brand being the most popular in France. The distributor's local competition would love to get their hands on the product, but the seller wisely supports the distributor and refuses to sell to anyone else in France. Enter a buyer with a huge EXW order for Paraguay, a country in which the exporter has no activity. Guess where the product really winds up. Guess whose distributor is furious.

Sellers should also be aware that the EXW rule does not obligate the buyer to export at all. Bogus export transactions could be diverted to the domestic market. This can be very disruptive for branded goods or those sold at substantial discount for export. A bogus export transaction could also have sales tax consequences.

U.S. importers face mirror image problems, as most countries have export control regulations of their own. Additionally, countries with value added taxation (VAT) regimes typically forgive this sales tax for exports. However, they require proof of export which can be difficult or impossible when the seller does not handle export clearance. Even importers with door-to-door transportation and local forwarders face the problem of loading the collecting conveyance.

Having explained how impractical EXW is for U.S. exports and imports, let me explain its importance as a basis for building towards more usable Incoterms® rules. The EXW price includes product and packaging only. (You may wonder why we didn't remove the packaging obligation from EXW in this revision too. As this depends so much on the kind of product, it is best left in. Be sure to include a separate line item price for any heroic export packing on your quotations.) Everything else is extra, including loading the collecting conveyance. By moving to other rules and adding line items for additional services provided (like forwarding, pre-carriage, main carriage, on-carriage, insurance, etc.), sellers can demonstrate what they are offering at what prices. Informed buyers appreciate such information.

Domestic use

EX Works can be appropriate for domestic transactions where there is no export clearance involved and unloading can be done by someone than the seller. Small package carriers immediately come to mind. There are also "self-loading" conveyances for situations like bulk commodity shipments (not to be confused with vessel loading as covered by the FOB Incoterms® rule). Also, some types of product are withdrawn rather than loaded.

[xxi] Incoterms® 2010 (ISBN 978-92-842-0080-1), ICC No. 720, ICC Publishing SA, Paris, France, available from ICC Publishing Inc., New York, NY

[xxii] Incoterms® 2010 (ISBN 978-92-842-0080-1), ICC No. 720, ICC Publishing SA, Paris, France, available from ICC Publishing Inc., New York, NY

PROFORMA INVOICE

EXPORTER Les Widgets de France Rue John-Pierre Robin 12 Strasbourg FRANCE	**PROFORMA INVOICE #** 8.1
	PROFORMA INVOICE DATE September 30, 2010
	PROFORMA VALIDITY DATE October 30, 2010
	EST'D SHIPMENT DATE Tomorrow
SOLD TO Widgets by Otto III Dean Haberkampstrasse Baden Baden GERMANY	**TERMS OF PAYMENT** Net 30 days
	SHIPMENT/DELIVERY TERMS EXW Rue John-Pierre Robin 12, Strasbourg, France, Incoterms 2010
SHIP TO Pick Up	**TITLE** Ownership transfers when payment is received by seller

QUANTITY	UNITS	DESCRIPTION OF MERCHANDISE	UNIT PRICE	TOTAL
40	Each	Bleu widgets	€ 100.00	4000.00

LAW & DISPUTE RESOLUTION: The U.N. Convention on Contracts for the International Sale of Goods (1980) shall apply to this offer and any resulting contract. Any disputes will be resolved by binding arbitration services of the International Chamber of Commerce.	**MERCHANDISE TOTAL**	€ 4000.00
	GRAND TOTAL EXW Strasbourg	€ 4000.00

PROFORMA INVOICE

EXPORTER Glotz Industries Inc 1492 Columbus Boulevard Fort Wayne, Indiana 12345-6789 USA	**PROFORMA INVOICE #** 8.2 **PROFORMA INVOICE DATE** September 30, 2010 **PROFORMA VALIDITY DATE** October 30, 2010 **EST'D SHIPMENT DATE** October 15, 2010
SOLD TO Widgets by Otto III Dean Haberkampstrasse Baden Baden GERMANY	**TERMS OF PAYMENT** Net 30 days **SHIPMENT/DELIVERY TERMS** EXW 1492 Columbus Blvd., Fort Wayne, Indiana, USA, Incoterms 2010
SHIP TO Pick Up	**TITLE** Ownership transfers when payment is received by seller

QUANTITY	UNITS	DESCRIPTION OF MERCHANDISE	UNIT PRICE	TOTAL
20	Each	Blue widgets	100.00	2000.00

LAW & DISPUTE RESOLUTION: The U.N. Convention on Contracts for the International Sale of Goods (1980) shall apply to this offer and any resulting contract. Any disputes will be resolved by binding arbitration services of the International Chamber of Commerce.	**MERCHANDISE TOTAL** Export Packing	**US$** 2000.00 123.00
	GRAND TOTAL EXW Fort Wayne	**US$** 2123.00

PROFORMA INVOICE

EXPORTER Glotz Industries Inc 1492 Columbus Boulevard Fort Wayne, Indiana 12345-6789 USA	**PROFORMA INVOICE #** 8.3 **PROFORMA INVOICE DATE** May 25, 2010 **PROFORMA VALIDITY DATE** June 25, 2010 **EST'D SHIPMENT DATE** June 5, 2010
SOLD TO Gordie's Good Widgets 1 Carl Crewson Street North Bay, Ontario CANADA	**TERMS OF PAYMENT** Net 30 days **SHIPMENT/DELIVERY TERMS** EXW 1492 Columbus Blvd., Fort Wayne, Indiana, USA, Incoterms 2010
SHIP TO Pick Up	**TITLE** Ownership transfers when payment is received by seller

QUANTITY	UNITS	DESCRIPTION OF MERCHANDISE	UNIT PRICE	TOTAL
40	Each	Blue widgets	100.00	4000.00

LAW & DISPUTE RESOLUTION: The U.N. Convention on Contracts for the International Sale of Goods (1980) shall apply to this offer and any resulting contract. Any disputes will be resolved by binding arbitration services of the International Chamber of Commerce.	**MERCHANDISE TOTAL**	**US$** 4000.00
	GRAND TOTAL EXW Fort Wayne	**US$** 4000.00

PROFORMA INVOICE

SELLER Glotz Industries Inc 1492 Columbus Boulevard Fort Wayne, Indiana 12345-6789 USA	**PROFORMA INVOICE #** 8.4 **PROFORMA INVOICE DATE** September 30, 2010 **PROFORMA VALIDITY DATE** October 30, 2010 **EST'D SHIPMENT DATE** October 1, 2010
SOLD TO Riddle Enterprises 1066 Campbell Ct. Seattle, Washington USA	**TERMS OF PAYMENT** Net 30 days **SHIPMENT/DELIVERY TERMS** EXW 1492 Columbus Boulevard, Fort Wayne, Indiana, USA, Incoterms 2010
SHIP TO Same as SOLD TO by UPS Next Day Air	**TITLE** Ownership transfers when payment is received by seller

QUANTITY	UNITS	DESCRIPTION OF MERCHANDISE	UNIT PRICE	TOTAL
2	Each	Blue widgets	100.00	200.00

LAW & DISPUTE RESOLUTION: The law of the state of Indiana shall apply to this offer and any resulting contract. Any disputes will be resolved by binding arbitration services of the American Arbitration Association.	**MERCHANDISE TOTAL**	**US$** 200.00
	GRAND TOTAL EXW Fort Wayne	**US$** 200.00

Chapter 9 - Free Carrier

Abbreviation: FCA
Transport mode: all
Contract type: shipment
Place: somewhere on the seller's side of subsequent transportation

Free Carrier (FCA) is the most versatile of the F-Group Incoterms® rules. It can be used with any mode of transportation, and there are two possible alternatives, both on the seller's side:
the seller's premises ,
or,
anywhere else on the seller's side after pre-carriage and prior to any subsequent transportation.

At the seller's premises
All the seller needs to do is have the goods suitably packaged at the agreed time, and promptly notify the buyer that they are ready. The seller merely supplies the goods without any transportation arrangements, and it falls to the buyer to arrange them. Unlike EXW, the seller is responsible for loading the collecting conveyance, and delivers once this is done. Also, unlike EXW, the seller is obligated to handle any export clearance.

Anywhere else on the seller's side
For international use, the other place is likely a buyer-appointed carrier's terminal or forwarder's warehouse, and the seller is obligated to handle export clearance. For domestic trade, it is anywhere on the seller's side prior to any main carriage, perhaps a consolidation point. The FCA rule should not be used with a final destination, as the seller has no (main) carriage obligation under A3. For both domestic and international use when the accompanying place is other than the seller's premises, the seller is responsible for the condition of the goods and the transportation costs until they get there. Once the pre-carriage conveyance arrives at the specified place ready for unloading, the seller has delivered. The seller is not responsible for unloading the delivering conveyance. It must also notify the buyer either that the goods have been delivered or that the buyer-appointed party has failed to receive them.

The logic behind loading and unloading responds to the simple question: "which party is best equipped to handle the task." The seller has the people and forklift equipment available to load when the place is its own premises. When it is another place, the seller loads, but the party at the other place (for instance, a buyer-appointed carrier's terminal) would have the necessary equipment for unloading.

FCA is designed for delivery to occur on the seller's side prior to subsequent (main) carriage. It is not a substitute for an arrival rule like DAP, DAT or DDP. FCA is used for shipment contracts. This is obvious when FCA is accompanied by the seller's premises. Even when the accompanying place is elsewhere, the seller is handing over the goods to a buyer-appointed party for subsequent transportation, which is why A3 of the FCA rule states that the seller is not responsible for carriage. It is also the reason FCA should not be used when there is no subsequent transportation.

We will cover the two FCA versions separately with examples of each.

Note: Although arranging for any main carriage is strictly speaking a buyer obligation, sellers sometimes take on this task for the buyers at the buyers' risk and cost. The resulting documentation would be a freight-collect transport document, with carriage arrangements made by the seller for the account of the buyer.

FCA + Seller's premises

This is what we really meant when we used the old UCC F.O.B. Factory term! The stipulated place is where transportation begins, often the seller's own premises. This should be described in geographic terms in as much detail as possible, including addresses, such as FCA 1150 South McCord Rd., Holland, Ohio, Incoterms® 2010.

FCA + seller's premises works well when buyers have contracted for pre-carriage transportation or pick the goods up themselves as the seller loads the collecting conveyance.

International shipments are accommodated, since sellers are responsible for export clearance. Sellers need to exercise due diligence as they are not in a position to know the disposition of their shipments once they depart. Savvy U.S. exporters use the Census Bureau's FTRs to their advantage by obtaining written authorizations from their buyers to file the EEIs. They then insist that the buyer-appointed forwarders and carriers provide the transportation information in writing to enable them to do the filing. The buyers should have no reluctance to provide authorizations since under the FCA rule they have already agreed that the sellers do this. In fact, any buyer reluctance should be treated with suspicion, as it would be contrary to the sales contract.

BUYER-SELLER RESPONSIBILITIES

The following is a short list of responsibilities.

1. **Goods and Payment**
   The seller must have the goods available when promised, suitably packaged, and must promptly notify the buyer that they are available for pickup. The buyer must pay the seller. FCA may be used with all means of transport. For this reason, the seller's obligation to suitably package may largely depend upon the buyer making the seller aware of the transportation arrangements, particularly for export transactions. For instance, if the buyer gives the seller reason to believe that shipment will be made by air, and changes plans without the seller's knowledge, the seller would not know to provide the robust packaging required for ocean shipments. **Also, the packaging definition found in Incoterms® 2010[xxiii] states that these rules do not cover container stowage and that this should be covered elsewhere in the sales contract. This is new.**
2. **Loading the collecting conveyance**
   The seller is responsible for loading the collecting conveyance.
3. **Pre-carriage**
   The seller is not responsible. This presents no particular problem with domestic shipments. No particular problem for international shipments either, provided the buyer has a "door-to-

somewhere" carriage contract. When this isn't the case, foreign buyers could be put in an awkward situation of trying to arrange pre-carriage in the seller's country.

4. **Export clearance**
   This is a seller responsibility under this rule.
5. **Other hoops and hurdles**
   The parties must work together on cargo security information. This usually means one party telling the other what is required and the other party providing it. Since security regulations change often and vary from country to country and from one transport mode to another, Incoterms® rules are limited to making the parties aware that they must be addressed. This is covered in A10-B10.
6. **Insurance**
   Neither party is required to insure under FCA. However, common sense dictates otherwise, and insurance should be addressed outside of the rule. This is particularly important for buyers because risk of loss passes from the seller to the buyer when the seller delivers, which happens prior to any transportation.
7. **Documentary implications**
   a. Commercial Documents: The seller should provide a commercial invoice, a packing list, and any other commercial documents cited in the sales contract.
   b. Transport Documents: The seller is not required to provide a transport document. However, in order to prove delivery it may require the collecting conveyance to provide a receipt. Since the seller is required to load, a freight collect truck bill of lading prepared by the seller but signed by the driver is typical.
   c. Export Control Documentation: The seller is obligated to handle export clearance. In a routed transaction, as the USPPI, the seller is obligated at a minimum to provide company and product specific information to the buyer-appointed agent for EEI filing. Proactive sellers who obtain buyer authorizations and file the EEIs will have an electronic record of filing. With the possible exception of specific export licenses, there is no longer a paper document involved as U.S. export reporting is done electronically.
   d. Import Entry Documentation: This is a buyer obligation. However, A10 requires the seller to provide assistance at the buyer's request, risk and cost.
8. **Payment terms considerations**
   By definition, the buyer must arrange for pick-up at the stipulated place under this version of the FCA Incoterms® rule. It then follows that the seller must be prepared to turn the goods over at that place. This means there's no way to use documents to restrict possession of the goods. This argues strongly for open account or payment in advance. It is possible that a freight collect truck bill of lading document or a forwarder's receipt could be used to trigger payment under a letter of credit. It is also possible that a negotiable freight collect received for shipment multimodal transportation document could be used both for letters of credit and documentary collections. However, as the seller is not contracting for carriage, the risk exists that the buyer-appointed carrier or forwarder may not follow any seller-provided instructions, or may refuse to provide the needed document to the seller.

STORY LINE

Otto and Andre

Otto is a young importer of widgets located in Baden Baden, Germany. Andre is Otto's French widget supplier, located in Strasbourg, France, quite near the German border. Whenever Otto sends a common carrier truck, the parties agree to use the FCA Incoterms® rule accompanied by the address of Andre's factory as shown in Andre's proforma invoice 9.1. Otto has negotiated an excellent freight rate. Andre prepares Otto's order for shipment and loads the truck when it arrives. All carriage is handled by the same trucking company. There are no export clearance or import clearance formalities between France and Germany as both are EU members.

Otto and Glotz

As we saw in Chapter 7, Otto wishes to purchase from Glotz Industries, a Fort Wayne widget manufacturer. Although the parties have enjoyed a longstanding relationship, neither has access to the way business had been conducted in the past. Both are literally starting from scratch. As shown in proforma invoice 9.2, Glotz requoted using the FCA Incoterms® rule after Otto rejected Glotz's EXW proposal. This relieved Otto of any loading or export clearance obligation, but the idea of making transportation arrangements from a factory in an unknown part of a foreign country was still too much for Otto to accept. He again requested Glotz to assume more of the transaction burden by quoting under a different Incoterms® rule. We'll see the results in subsequent chapters.

Gordie and Glotz

This is the way Gordie normally purchases (when he is not visiting Indianapolis). He has negotiated an excellent door-to-door freight rate. Because of cabotage agreements between the U.S. and Canada, the same truck line that picks up at Glotz's factory delivers at Gordie's warehouse. See Glotz's proforma invoice 9.3. This situation parallels Otto and Andre above.

Riddle and Glotz

Similar to Andre and Glotz and Gordie and Glotz above. See Glotz's proforma invoice 9.4

FCA + Other Point on Seller's Side

This version of the FCA Incoterms® rule works well when the seller delivers to a location other than its premises on the seller's side of subsequent carriage. Examples include a buyer-appointed carrier, a buyer-appointed forwarder or a buyer-appointed consolidator. When used for international sales we say "seller's side" to mean a location often in the seller's own country. Domestically, it would be also be anywhere on the seller's side of any subsequent carriage. Because FCA A3 specifies that the seller has no (main) carriage obligation, it should not be used with a final destination such as the buyer's premises. For both international and domestic use the seller arranges for pre-carriage transportation to the agreed place, and remains responsible for the condition of the contract goods until they arrive there. Delivery occurs when the delivering conveyance arrives at the agreed place ready for unloading. The reason is that the buyer-appointed carrier, forwarder, etc. would normally have people and equipment at its disposal to unload at its premises.

The place should be described in geographic terms in as much detail as possible, including addresses, such as Transair Lines, Building 2, Toledo Express Airport, Incoterms® 2010.

International shipments are accommodated, since sellers are responsible for export clearance. Exporters need to exercise due diligence as they are not in a position to know the disposition of their shipments once they are delivered. However, as they are usually bringing them to a buyer-appointed carrier or forwarder, they are a transport leg closer to the actual export than is the case with EXW or FCA + seller's premises. It should be fairly easy to check the reputation of the carrier or forwarder. Savvy U.S. exporters use the Census Bureau's FTRs to their advantage by obtaining written authorizations from their buyers to file the EEIs. They then insist that the buyer-appointed forwarders and carriers provide the transportation information in writing to enable them to do the filing. The buyers should have no reluctance to provide authorizations since under the FCA rule they have already agreed that the sellers do this. In fact, any buyer reluctance should be treated with suspicion as it would be contrary to the sales contract.

FCA + another place on the seller's side works well when sellers provide or contract for pre-carriage transportation. As mentioned at the start of this chapter, FCA should not be used as a substitute for an arrival rule such as DAP, DAT or DDP.

BUYER-SELLER RESPONSIBILITIES

The following is a short list of responsibilities

1. **Goods and Payment**

The seller must have the goods available when promised, suitably packaged, must promptly notify the buyer that they are ready, and must transport them to the agreed place on the seller's side. The buyer must pay the seller. FCA may be used with all means of transport. For this reason, the seller's obligation to suitably package may largely depend upon the buyer making the seller aware of the subsequent transportation arrangements, particularly for export. This may be obvious because of the agreed delivery place (seaport, airport, container consolidator, etc.). **Note: the packaging definition found in Incoterms® 2010 states that these rules do not cover container stowage and that this should be covered elsewhere in the sales contract. This is new.**

2. **Loading and unloading**
   The seller is responsible for loading the delivering conveyance, but the buyer is responsible for unloading.
3. **Pre-carriage**
   This is a seller responsibility under this FCA version.
4. **Export clearance**
   This is a seller responsibility under this rule.
5. **Other hoops and hurdles**
   The parties must work together on cargo security information. This usually means one party telling the other what is required and the other party providing it. Since security regulations change often and vary from country to country and from one transport mode to another, Incoterms® rules are limited to making the parties aware that they must be addressed. This is covered in A10-B10.
6. **Insurance**
   Neither party is required to insure under FCA. However, common sense dictates otherwise, and insurance should be addressed outside of the rule. This is because sellers bear the risk of loss through pre-carriage, while buyers are at risk thereafter.
7. **Documentary implications**
   a. Commercial Documents: The seller should provide a commercial invoice, a packing list, and any other commercial documents cited in the sales contract.
   b. Transport Documents: The seller should provide evidence that the contract goods were received at the agreed place.
   c. Export Control Documentation: The seller is obligated to handle export clearance. In a routed transaction, as the USPPI, the seller is obligated at a minimum to provide company and product specific information to the buyer-appointed agent for EEI filing. Proactive sellers who obtain buyer authorizations and file the EEIs will have an electronic record of filing. With the possible exception of specific export licenses, there is no longer a paper document involved as U.S. export reporting is done electronically.
   d. Import Entry Documentation: This is a buyer obligation. However, A10 requires the seller to provide assistance at the buyer's request, risk and cost.
8. **Payment terms considerations**
   By definition, the seller must arrange for delivery at the stipulated place under this version of the FCA Incoterms® rule. It then follows that the seller must be prepared to turn the goods over at that place. This means there's no way to use documents to restrict possession of the goods (although COD is a remote possibility). This argues strongly for open account or payment in advance. It is possible that a forwarder's receipt could be used to trigger payment under a letter of credit. It is also possible that a negotiable freight collect received for shipment multimodal transportation document could be used both for letters of credit and documentary collections. However, as the seller is not contracting for subsequent carriage, the risk exists that the buyer-

appointed carrier or forwarder may not follow any seller-provided instructions, or may refuse to provide the needed document to the seller.

STORY LINE

Otto and Andre
Otto is a young importer of widgets located in Baden Baden, Germany. Andre is Otto's French widget supplier, located in Strasbourg, France, quite near the German border. Because the two places are so close to each other, they never use subsequent carriers, and therefore do not use this FCA version.

Otto and Glotz
As we saw in Chapter 7, Otto wishes to purchase from Glotz Industries, a Fort Wayne widget manufacturer. Both are literally starting from scratch. As shown in proforma invoice 9.5, Glotz agreed to arrange and pay for pre-carriage to an international carrier at O'Hare airport. This relieved Otto of any loading or export clearance obligation as well as transportation in the U.S. All he has to do is arrange main carriage, import clearance and on-carriage which he should be able to do from Germany. The question is, at what cost. Otto replied that this quotation was being considered, but that he would appreciate Glotz's shopping around for an air freight quotation. This will bring us to the next chapter, CPT.

Gordie and Glotz
Because of cabotage agreements between the U.S. and Canada, the same truck line that picks up at Glotz's factory delivers at Gordie's warehouse. For this reason, Gordie never uses this FCA version. Again, this situation parallels Andre-Glotz above.

Jerry and Glotz
As mentioned in Chapter 7, Jerry Prieto imports Glotz's widgets for use in his Monterrey battery factory. As shown in proforma 9.6, he always uses this FCA version, specifying his forwarder's Laredo Texas warehouse as the location. There are several reasons for this. First, Mexican import regulations require filing of all pertinent information and payment of duty before the "pedimento" (permission to import) is issued. This can take anywhere from days to weeks. To accommodate this, many border forwarders offer warehousing and customs brokerage services on both sides. Next, as of this writing, U.S. and Mexican trucks are not allowed to travel in each others' countries beyond locations near the border. Although it is possible to get "door-to-door" freight rates, there is a physical change of equipment at the border. Finally, many U.S. exporters are not comfortable with transit risk within Mexico.

Riddle and Glotz
As a large distributor, Riddle is constantly receiving different size shipments by different means. Ideally, they prefer to order monthly and in full truckload quantities. Very small urgently needed shipments travel next-day by small package carriers as seen in Chapter 8. There's a third alternative; less-than-truckload shipments that are not urgent enough for small package delivery but cannot await the usual monthly truckload shipment. Riddle has another supplier in South Bend, Indiana, from which it orders weekly truckload shipments. As shown in proforma 9.7, it sometimes asks Glotz to deliver there for consolidation and subsequent transportation to Seattle.

AMERICAN VIEWPOINT TO BOTH VERSIONS

International use
While the Incoterms® rule tasks the seller with export clearance, this can be at odds with local regulations.

Routed transactions: For U.S. exports, the Census Bureau's Foreign Trade Regulations require the party appointed by the buyer to file the Electronic Export Information (EEI). This usually translates to a buyer-appointed forwarder (or carrier as their roles are increasingly becoming interchangeable) . The seller, known as the United States Principal Party in Interest (USPPI), is required to provide this party with the company and product specific information necessary to file the EEI. In return, the USPPI is entitled only to written confirmation from this service provider with respect to the information it provided. The USPPI has no right to the transportation information in this situation as the EEI is confidential between the filer and Census.

As mentioned earlier and explained in more detail in Chapter 19, there is relief for exporters that prefer to file their EEIs in routed transactions rather than trusting service providers over which they have no control. An additional payoff is access to the transportation information. Savvy sellers use this to help their forwarders obtain lower freight costs and better service in order to gain control of future shipments.

There are a few other potential seller risks with all F-Group rules that stem from the buyer's contracting for main carriage with the carrier. This normally means that the buyer also appoints the forwarder. Both of these service providers would therefore follow instructions from the buyer rather than any they receive from the seller. This opens the possibility of diversion which could be an illegal shipment to a prohibited party or country. More likely would be commercial diversion to a non-restricted party or country other than the destination desired by the seller. Depending on the product, doing so may not violate export regulations but could seriously compromise the seller's distribution arrangements. Also, seller access to transportation documents could present a problem, particularly with document-driven payment terms.

Speaking of payment terms, don't be surprised to receive letters of credit calling for freight collect "on board ocean bills of lading," extending the beneficiary's risk through vessel loading. Many banks simply will not accept a "received for shipment" document, regardless of the fact that this agrees with the seller's FCA Incoterms® obligation. Others confuse the "on board-ness" with consignment instructions. (It is perfectly possible to have a negotiable received for shipment marine transportation document.) Unfortunately, as the buyer is contracting for main carriage, the seller who is beneficiary of such a letter of credit would be at risk for the loading operations of a carrier it did not choose and may never have chosen.

Another drawback is that each shipment made under F-Group Incoterms® rules is one more that isn't counted to the seller's credit in negotiating shippers' agreements. Service providers respect VOLUME above all. Shippers that control many shipments have, do, and always will pay lower freight costs and get better service than do less frequent shippers. Since the shipper is the party contracting for transportation with the carrier, the buyer is actually the shipper under F-Group rules.

U.S. importers do well with FCA. The fact that export clearance is a seller obligation makes it easier for suppliers in value added tax countries to claim refunds. Also, U.S. import duty is not payable on freight to get here, so the FCA price is usually the dutiable value. As we saw above, freight cost savings and superior carrier service accrue to buyers who control enough shipments to become large shippers. Finally, the "10+2" rule holds U.S. importers responsible for filing detailed information with Customs prior to vessel loading for most waterborne import shipments. Controlling the overseas forwarder really helps compliance.

Domestic use

FCA presents no problem for purely domestic transactions as long as it is not used with a final destination.

[xxiii] Incoterms® 2010 (ISBN 978-92-842-0080-1), ICC No. 720, ICC Publishing SA, Paris, France, available from ICC Publishing Inc., New York, NY

PROFORMA INVOICE

EXPORTER Les Widgets de France Rue John-Pierre Robin 12 Strasbourg FRANCE	**PROFORMA INVOICE #** 9.1 **PROFORMA INVOICE DATE** September 30, 2010 **PROFORMA VALIDITY DATE** October 30, 2010 **EST'D SHIPMENT DATE** October 4, 2010
SOLD TO Widgets by Otto III Dean Haberkampstrasse Baden Baden GERMANY	**TERMS OF PAYMENT** Net 30 days **SHIPMENT/DELIVERY TERMS** FCA Rue John-Pierre Robin 12, Strasbourg, France, Incoterms 2010
SHIP TO Pick Up	**TITLE** Ownership transfers when payment is received by seller

QUANTITY	UNITS	DESCRIPTION OF MERCHANDISE	UNIT PRICE	TOTAL
40	Each	Bleu widgets	€ 100.00	4000.00

LAW & DISPUTE RESOLUTION: The U.N. Convention on Contracts for the International Sale of Goods (1980) shall apply to this offer and any resulting contract. Any disputes will be resolved by binding arbitration services of the International Chamber of Commerce.	**MERCHANDISE TOTAL**	€ 4000.00
	GRAND TOTAL FCA Strasbourg	€ 4000.00

PROFORMA INVOICE

EXPORTER Glotz Industries Inc 1492 Columbus Boulevard Fort Wayne, Indiana 12345-6789 USA	**PROFORMA INVOICE #** 9.2 **PROFORMA INVOICE DATE** October 5, 2010 **PROFORMA VALIDITY DATE** November 5, 2010 **EST'D SHIPMENT DATE** October 20, 2010
SOLD TO Widgets by Otto III Dean Haberkampstrasse Baden Baden GERMANY	**TERMS OF PAYMENT** Net 30 days **SHIPMENT/DELIVERY TERMS** FCA 1492 Columbus Blvd., Fort Wayne, Indiana, USA, Incoterms 2010
SHIP TO Pick Up	**TITLE** Ownership transfers when payment is received by seller

QUANTITY	**UNITS**	**DESCRIPTION OF MERCHANDISE**	**UNIT PRICE**	**TOTAL**
20	Each	Blue widgets	100.00	2000.00

LAW & DISPUTE RESOLUTION: The U.N. Convention on Contracts for the International Sale of Goods (1980) shall apply to this offer and any resulting contract. Any disputes will be resolved by binding arbitration services of the International Chamber of Commerce.	**MERCHANDISE TOTAL** Export Packing	**US$** 2000.00 123.00
	GRAND TOTAL FCA Fort Wayne	**US$** 2123.00

PROFORMA INVOICE

EXPORTER Glotz Industries Inc 1492 Columbus Boulevard Fort Wayne, Indiana 12345-6789 USA	**PROFORMA INVOICE #** 9.3 **PROFORMA INVOICE DATE** September 30, 2010
	PROFORMA VALIDITY DATE October 30, 2010 **EST'D SHIPMENT DATE** October 8, 2010
SOLD TO Gordie's Good Widgets 1 Carl Crewson Street North Bay, Ontario CANADA	**TERMS OF PAYMENT** Net 30 days
	SHIPMENT/DELIVERY TERMS FCA 1492 Columbus Blvd., Fort Wayne, Indiana, USA, Incoterms 2010
SHIP TO Pick Up	**TITLE** Ownership transfers when payment is received by seller

QUANTITY	UNITS	DESCRIPTION OF MERCHANDISE	UNIT PRICE	TOTAL
40	Each	Blue widgets	100.00	4000.00

LAW & DISPUTE RESOLUTION: The U.N. Convention on Contracts for the International Sale of Goods (1980) shall apply to this offer and any resulting contract. Any disputes will be resolved by binding arbitration services of the International Chamber of Commerce.	**MERCHANDISE TOTAL**	**US$** 4000.00
	GRAND TOTAL FCA Fort Wayne	**US$** 4000.00

PROFORMA INVOICE

SELLER Glotz Industries Inc 1492 Columbus Boulevard Fort Wayne, Indiana 12345-6789 USA	**PROFORMA INVOICE #** 9.4 **PROFORMA INVOICE DATE** September 30, 2010 **PROFORMA VALIDITY DATE** October 30, 2010 **EST'D SHIPMENT DATE** October 8, 2010
SOLD TO Riddle Enterprises 1066 Campbell Ct. Seattle, Washington USA	**TERMS OF PAYMENT** Net 30 days **SHIPMENT/DELIVERY TERMS** FCA 1492 Columbus Boulevard, Fort Wayne, Indiana, USA, Incoterms 2010
SHIP TO Pick Up	**TITLE** Ownership transfers when payment is received by seller

QUANTITY	UNITS	DESCRIPTION OF MERCHANDISE	UNIT PRICE	TOTAL
450	Each	Blue widgets	89.00	40050.00

LAW & DISPUTE RESOLUTION: The law of the state of Indiana shall apply to this offer and any resulting contract. Any disputes will be resolved by binding arbitration services of the American Arbitration Association.	**MERCHANDISE TOTAL**	**US$** 40050.00
	GRAND TOTAL FCA Fort Wayne	**US$** 40,050.00

PROFORMA INVOICE

EXPORTER Glotz Industries Inc 1492 Columbus Boulevard Fort Wayne, Indiana 12345-6789 USA	**PROFORMA INVOICE #** 9.5
	PROFORMA INVOICE DATE October 7, 2010
	PROFORMA VALIDITY DATE November 7, 2010
	EST'D SHIPMENT DATE October 22, 2010
SOLD TO Widgets by Otto III Dean Haberkampstrasse Baden Baden GERMANY	**TERMS OF PAYMENT** Net 30 days
	SHIPMENT/DELIVERY TERMS FCA Air America Terminal 2, O'Hare Airport, Chicago, IL, USA, Incoterms 2010
SHIP TO Air America Terminal 2, O'Hare Airport, Chicago, IL, USA	**TITLE** Ownership transfers when payment is received by seller

QUANTITY	UNITS	DESCRIPTION OF MERCHANDISE	UNIT PRICE	TOTAL
20	Each	Blue widgets	100.00	2000.00

LAW & DISPUTE RESOLUTION: The U.N. Convention on Contracts for the International Sale of Goods (1980) shall apply to this offer and any resulting contract. Any disputes will be resolved by binding arbitration services of the International Chamber of Commerce.	**MERCHANDISE TOTAL** Export Packing Pre-carriage	**US$** 2000.00 123.00 138.00
	GRAND TOTAL FCA O'Hare Airport	**US$** 2261.00

PROFORMA INVOICE

EXPORTER Glotz Industries Inc 1492 Columbus Boulevard Fort Wayne, Indiana 12345-6789 USA	**PROFORMA INVOICE #** 9.6 **PROFORMA INVOICE DATE** September 30, 2010 **PROFORMA VALIDITY DATE** October 30, 2010 **EST'D SHIPMENT DATE** October 15, 2010
SOLD TO Baterias de Monterrey SA 55 Cantu Plaza Monterrey, NL, MEXICO	**TERMS OF PAYMENT** Net 30 days **SHIPMENT/DELIVERY TERMS** FCA 1836 Sam Houston Dr., Laredo, Texas, USA, Incoterms 2010
SHIP TO Rapido y Corecto Forwarding 1836 Sam Houston Dr. Laredo, Texas USA	**TITLE** Ownership transfers when payment is received by seller

QUANTITY	UNITS	DESCRIPTION OF MERCHANDISE	UNIT PRICE	TOTAL
40	Each	Blue widgets	100.00	4000.00

LAW & DISPUTE RESOLUTION: The U.N. Convention on Contracts for the International Sale of Goods (1980) shall apply to this offer and any resulting contract. Any disputes will be resolved by binding arbitration services of the International Chamber of Commerce.	**MERCHANDISE TOTAL** Pre-carriage	**US$** 4000.00 872.00
	GRAND TOTAL FCA Laredo, Texas	**US$** 4872.00

PROFORMA INVOICE

SELLER Glotz Industries Inc 1492 Columbus Boulevard Fort Wayne, Indiana 12345-6789 USA	**PROFORMA INVOICE #** 9.7 **PROFORMA INVOICE DATE** September 30, 2010 **PROFORMA VALIDITY DATE** October 30, 2010 **EST'D SHIPMENT DATE** October 8, 2010
SOLD TO Riddle Enterprises 1066 Campbell Ct. Seattle, Washington USA	**TERMS OF PAYMENT** Net 30 days **SHIPMENT/DELIVERY TERMS** FCA 1 Touchdown Dr, South Bend, Indiana, USA, Incoterms 2010
SHIP TO Riddle Enterprises c/o Othersupplier Inc 1 Touchdown Dr South Bend, Indiana, USA	**TITLE** Ownership transfers when payment is received by seller

QUANTITY	UNITS	DESCRIPTION OF MERCHANDISE	UNIT PRICE	TOTAL
14	Each	Blue widgets	100.00	1400.00

LAW & DISPUTE RESOLUTION: The law of the state of Indiana shall apply to this offer and any resulting contract. Any disputes will be resolved by binding arbitration services of the American Arbitration Association.	**MERCHANDISE TOTAL** Pre-carriage	**US$** 1400.00 82.00
	GRAND TOTAL FCA South Bend	**US$** 1482.00

Chapter 10 - Carriage Paid To

Abbreviation: CPT
Transport mode: all
Contract type: shipment
Place: somewhere on the buyer's side of transportation

Carriage Paid To (CPT) and its first cousin, Carriage and Insurance Paid To (CIP) are the most versatile of the C-Group Incoterms® rules. The difference between the two is that under CPT, no one is required to insure (although the buyer should have strong commercial interest in doing so outside the rule). Both rules can be used with any mode of transportation. The place must be on the buyer's side of transportation for which the seller contracts. For international trade, possibilities include an arrival point (port, airport, etc.) or anywhere else on the buyer's side that the parties agree, including the buyer's premises. For domestic trade, it's at the end of transportation contracted for by the seller and agreed by the parties. Whatever place the parties select should be spelled out in as much detail as possible, including street addresses when available.

Sellers should carefully contract for transportation to match the agreed point at the agreed place, since buyers are not required to reimburse them for any additional costs beyond that point. This omnimodal rule is so versatile that the destination place cannot be set as a default. For instance, with vessel shipments, unloading can involve terminal handling and other such costs which may not apply to other transport modes like small package carriers. Since there is no consistency as to how and to whom carriers levy these charges, the parties should address this in their sales contract and sellers should contract for transportation accordingly.

CPT may be used with single carrier or multimodal transportation.

For international trade, CPT works particularly well when the seller contracts for door-to-somewhere (door, port, airport whatever) transportation. The reason is that the default position is that the **seller delivers by handing over the contract goods to the FIRST carrier**. When the first carrier is part of a carriage contract written on a door-to-somewhere-on-the-buyer's-side basis, the buyer should be able to claim on the main carrier even for mishaps that occur in pre-carriage. By contrast, let's suppose there are separate contracts for pre-carriage and main carriage. If there is loss or damage to the goods in pre-carriage, the foreign buyer is left in the unenviable position of trying to claim on the pre-carrier which is located in the seller's country. The seller is out of the picture as its risk ended with delivery to the pre-carrier. For an example, please see the American Viewpoint section of this chapter.

Ending the seller's risk at the first carrier may seem odd at first as under CPT the seller selects and contracts with the carrier. However, it is consistent with Article 67 of the United Nations Convention Contracts for the International Sale of Goods (CISG). Also, the first carrier provision was included in the

CPT rule since it was created in Incoterms 1990. Realizing that the risk transfer point may not be obvious to persons not already familiar with Incoterms® use, **Incoterms® 2010** [xxiv] **goes out of its way to point this out in the new Guidance Notes for these rules.** Parties in their sales contracts may agree that delivery will happen in a different place, such as when the goods are handed over to the main carrier. They may also agree to use a different Incoterms® rule altogether, such as DAP.

The same risk is of course present in domestic use. However, much of our domestic transportation is done on a door-to-door basis, and this default situation would occur only when more than one contract of carriage is involved. Also, both the domestic buyer and the pre-carrier are here.

International shipments are accommodated since sellers are responsible for export clearance.

Since the seller is contracting for carriage, it usually also appoints the forwarder for international transactions. This enables the seller to provide instructions to these parties without the risk of their following any conflicting instructions from the buyer.

BUYER-SELLER RESPONSIBILITIES

The following is a short list of responsibilities.

1. **Goods and Payment**
   The seller must ship the goods when promised, and must promptly notify the buyer that they have done so. The buyer must pay the seller. Since the seller is arranging transport, it should be aware of what packaging is needed. **However, the packaging definition found in Incoterms® 2010 states that these rules do not cover container stowage and that this should be covered elsewhere in the sales contract. This is new.**
2. **Loading and unloading**
   The seller is responsible for loading, and the buyer is responsible for unloading.
3. **Pre-carriage and main carriage (and on-carriage?)**
   The seller is responsible for payment of carriage to the agreed place. However, the default position is that the seller delivers by handing over the goods to the first carrier, which could cause problems unless carriage is contracted on a "door-to-somewhere" basis.
4. **Export clearance**
   This is a seller responsibility under this rule.
5. **Other hoops and hurdles**
   The parties must work together on cargo security information. This usually means one party telling the other what is required and the other party providing it. Since security regulations change often and vary from country to country and from one transport mode to another, Incoterms® rules are limited to making the parties aware that they must be addressed. This is covered in A10-B10.
6. **Insurance**
   Neither party is required to insure under CPT. However, common sense dictates otherwise, and the buyer should consider insurance outside of the rule because the risk of loss passes from the seller to the buyer at the first carrier.

7. **Documentary implications**
   a. Commercial Documents: The seller should provide a commercial invoice, a packing list, and any other commercial documents cited in the sales contract.
   b. Transport Documents: The seller must provide a freight-prepaid transport document if requested by the buyer.
   c. Export Control Documentation: The seller is obligated to handle export clearance under both CPT and the Foreign Trade Regulations. With the possible exception of specific export licenses, there is no longer a paper document involved as U.S. export reporting is done electronically.
   d. Import Entry Documentation: This is a buyer obligation. However, A10 requires the seller to provide assistance at the buyer's request, risk and cost.
8. **Payment terms considerations**
   By definition, the seller must arrange and pay for carriage to the agreed place. This means the seller is in a position to require the forwarder and carrier to provide transport documentation to its specifications, and will have access to them for use in both letters of credit and documentary collections.

STORY LINE

Otto and Andre

Otto is a young importer of widgets located in Baden Baden, Germany. Andre is Otto's French widget supplier, located in Strasbourg, France, quite near the German border. Although Otto has negotiated very good freight rates with a truck line serving Strasbourg and Baden Baden, Andre has an even better rate with a small package carrier which they use for very small shipments and next-day service. See proforma 10.1

Otto and Glotz

As we saw in Chapter 7, Otto wishes to purchase from Glotz Industries, a Fort Wayne widget manufacturer. Both are literally starting from scratch. After Otto rejected Glotz's EXW proposal, Glotz requoted using the FCA Incoterms® rule. Otto requested another quotation on a freight-paid basis for comparison, and Glotz quoted CPT. See proforma 10.2

Gordie and Glotz

Occasionally, Glotz can obtain a "sweetheart" freight rate that beats anything Gordie can come up with. Because of cabotage agreements between the U.S. and Canada, the same truck line that picks up at Glotz's factory delivers at Gordie's warehouse. See Glotz's proforma invoice 10.3.

Riddle and Glotz

Riddle always gets lower freight costs, and never purchases on a freight-prepaid basis.

The unloading logic is the same as found in FCA + location other than seller's premises, as the buyer is normally better positioned to unload than is the remote seller.

International use

This Incoterms® rule tasks the seller with export clearance. For U.S. exporters, this is consistent with the Foreign Trade Regulations. The seller, known as the United States Principal Party in Interest (USPPI), is required to file the EEI or appoint an agent to do so, usually a seller-appointed forwarder. As the USPPI is contracting for transportation, it will have the necessary transportation information to file.

Delivery at the first carrier can cause problems for inexperienced users when pre-carriage is contracted independently of main carriage. Here's an extreme example. A "mom & pop" truck line was transporting an expensive yacht to a seaport for shipment against a port-to-port contract of main carriage. The truck crashed on the Indiana Toll Road and never reached the port. Sadly, mom, pop, the truck and the yacht are no more. Upon whom does the foreign buyer claim?

Since both the carrier and presumably the forwarder are working for the seller, there should be no problem obtaining documents necessary to make payment terms work. However, don't be surprised to receive letters of credit calling for "on board ocean bills of lading," extending the beneficiary's risk through vessel loading. Many banks simply will not accept a "received for shipment" document, regardless of the fact that this agrees with the seller's CPT Incoterms® obligation. Others confuse the "on board-ness" with consignment instructions. It is perfectly possible to have a negotiable received for shipment marine transportation document. Fortunately, as the seller is contracting for main carriage, it is not unreasonable that it be responsible for the carrier's loading obligations.

Another seller advantage is that each shipment made under C-Group Incoterms® rules is another that is counted to its credit in negotiating shippers' agreements. Since the seller is the party contracting for transportation with the carrier, it is the shipper. Service providers respect VOLUME above all. Shippers that control many shipments have, do, and always will pay lower freight costs and get better service than less frequent shippers.

Experienced U.S. importers may prefer to buy on an F-Group term unless their suppliers offer exceptionally attractive freight costs. If this is the case, consider holding the seller responsible for the carrier it chooses by requesting DAT or DAP rather than C-Group rules. These rules also take the "first carrier" situation off the table. In any case, insist on proof of what the freight costs are such as a rated transport document to avoid paying import duty on inbound freight costs.

Domestic use

Except for buyers attempting to achieve large shipper status, CPT presents no problem for purely domestic transactions.

[xxiv] Incoterms® 2010 (ISBN 978-92-842-0080-1), ICC No. 720, ICC Publishing SA, Paris, France, available from ICC Publishing Inc., New York, NY

PROFORMA INVOICE

EXPORTER Les Widgets de France Rue John-Pierre Robin 12 Strasbourg FRANCE	**PROFORMA INVOICE #** 10.1 **PROFORMA INVOICE DATE** October 2, 2010 **PROFORMA VALIDITY DATE** November 2, 2010 **EST'D SHIPMENT DATE** October 6, 2010
SOLD TO Widgets by Otto III Dean Haberkampstrasse Baden Baden GERMANY	**TERMS OF PAYMENT** Net 30 days **SHIPMENT/DELIVERY TERMS** CPT Dean Haberkampstrasse, Baden Baden, Germany, Incoterms 2010
SHIP TO Same as SOLD TO	**TITLE** Ownership transfers when payment is received by seller

QUANTITY	UNITS	DESCRIPTION OF MERCHANDISE	UNIT PRICE	TOTAL
2	Each	Bleu widgets	€ 100.00	200.00

LAW & DISPUTE RESOLUTION: The U.N. Convention on Contracts for the International Sale of Goods (1980) shall apply to this offer and any resulting contract. Any disputes will be resolved by binding arbitration services of the International Chamber of Commerce.	**MERCHANDISE TOTAL** Freight	€ 200.00 32.00
	GRAND TOTAL CPT Baden Baden	€ 232.00

PROFORMA INVOICE

EXPORTER Glotz Industries Inc 1492 Columbus Boulevard Fort Wayne, Indiana 12345-6789 USA	**PROFORMA INVOICE #** 10.2 **PROFORMA INVOICE DATE** October 15, 2010 **PROFORMA VALIDITY DATE** November 15, 2010 **EST'D SHIPMENT DATE** November 1, 2010
SOLD TO Widgets by Otto III Dean Haberkampstrasse Baden Baden GERMANY	**TERMS OF PAYMENT** Net 30 days **SHIPMENT/DELIVERY TERMS** CPT Air America Terminal, Frankfurt Airport, Frankfurt, Germany, Incoterms 2010
SHIP TO Air America Terminal, Frankfurt Airport Frankfurt GERMANY	**TITLE** Ownership transfers when payment is received by seller

QUANTITY	UNITS	DESCRIPTION OF MERCHANDISE	UNIT PRICE	TOTAL
20	Each	Blue widgets	100.00	2000.00

LAW & DISPUTE RESOLUTION: The U.N. Convention on Contracts for the International Sale of Goods (1980) shall apply to this offer and any resulting contract. Any disputes will be resolved by binding arbitration services of the International Chamber of Commerce.	**MERCHANDISE TOTAL** Export Packing Pre-carriage Air Freight Forwarding	**US$** 2000.00 123.00 138.00 521.00 100.00
	GRAND TOTAL CPT Frankfurt	**US$** 2882.00

PROFORMA INVOICE

EXPORTER
Glotz Industries Inc
1492 Columbus Boulevard
Fort Wayne, Indiana 12345-6789
USA

PROFORMA INVOICE #
10.3

PROFORMA INVOICE DATE
October 15, 2010

PROFORMA VALIDITY DATE
November 15, 2010

EST'D SHIPMENT DATE
October 19, 2010

SOLD TO
Gordie's Good Widgets
1 Carl Crewson Street
North Bay, Ontario
CANADA

TERMS OF PAYMENT
Net 30 days

SHIPMENT/DELIVERY TERMS
CPT 1 Carl Crewson Street, North Bay, Ontario, Canada, Incoterms 2010

SHIP TO
Same as SOLD TO

TITLE
Ownership transfers when payment is received by seller

QUANTITY	UNITS	DESCRIPTION OF MERCHANDISE	UNIT PRICE	TOTAL
40	Each	Blue widgets	100.00	4000.00

LAW & DISPUTE RESOLUTION: The U.N. Convention on Contracts for the International Sale of Goods (1980) shall apply to this offer and any resulting contract. Any disputes will be resolved by binding arbitration services of the International Chamber of Commerce.

MERCHANDISE TOTAL	**US$** 4000.00
Freight	392.00
GRAND TOTAL CPT North Bay	**US$** 4392.00

Chapter 11 - Carriage and Insurance Paid To

Abbreviation: CIP
Transport mode: all
Contract type: shipment
Place: somewhere on the buyer's side of transportation

Carriage and Insurance Paid To (CIP) and its first cousin, Carriage Paid To (CPT) are the most versatile of the C-Group Incoterms® rules. The difference between the two is that under CIP the seller is required to insure. Both rules can be used with any mode of transportation. The place must be on the buyer's side of transportation for which the seller contracts. For international trade, possibilities include an arrival point (port, airport, etc.) or anywhere else on the buyer's side that the parties agree, including the buyer's premises. For domestic trade, it's at the end of transportation contracted for by the seller and agreed by the parties. Whatever place the parties select should be spelled out in as much detail as possible, including street addresses when available.

Sellers should carefully contract for transportation to match the agreed point at the agreed place, since buyers are not required to reimburse them for any additional costs beyond that point. This omnimodal rule is so versatile that the destination place cannot be set as a default. For instance, with vessel shipments, unloading can involve terminal handling and other such costs which may not apply to other transport modes like small package carriers. Since there is no consistency as to how and to whom carriers levy these charges, the parties should address this in their sales contract and sellers should contract for transportation accordingly.

CIP may be used with single carrier or multimodal transportation.

For international trade, CIP works particularly well when the seller contracts for door-to-somewhere (door, port, airport whatever) transportation. The reason is that the default position is that the **seller delivers by handing over the contract goods to the FIRST carrier**. When the first carrier is part of a carriage contract written on a door-to-somewhere-on-the-buyer's-side basis, the buyer should be able able to claim on the main carrier even for mishaps that occur in pre-carriage. By contrast, let's suppose there are separate contracts for pre-carriage and main carriage. If there is loss or damage to the goods in pre-carriage, the foreign buyer is left in the unenviable position of trying to claim on a pre-carrier located in the seller's country. The seller is out of the picture, as its risk ended with delivery to the pre-carrier. For an example, please see the American Viewpoint section of this chapter.

Ending the seller's risk at the first carrier may seem odd at first as under CIP the seller selects and contracts with the carrier. However, it is consistent with Article 67 of the United Nations Convention Contracts for the International Sale of Goods (CISG). Also, the first carrier provision was included in the CIP rule since it was created in Incoterms 1990. Realizing that the risk transfer point may not be obvious to persons not already familiar with Incoterms® use, **Incoterms® 2010** [xxv] **goes out of its way to**

point this out in the new Guidance Notes for these rules. Parties in their sales contracts may agree that delivery will happen in a different place, such as when the goods are handed over to the main carrier. They may also agree to use a different Incoterms® rule altogether, such as DAP.

The fact that the seller provides insurance may take some of the sting out of the first carrier situation, as long as the coverage is adequate.

The same risk is of course present in domestic use. However, much of our domestic transportation is done on a door-to-door basis, and this default situation would occur only when more than one contract of carriage is involved. Also, both the domestic buyer and the pre-carrier are here.

International shipments are accommodated since sellers are responsible for export clearance.

Since the seller is contracting for carriage, it usually also appoints the forwarder for international transactions. This enables the seller to provide instructions to these parties without the risk of their following any conflicting instructions from the buyer.

The CIP rule stipulates that the seller must provide insurance, but limits this obligation to minimum cover unless the parties agree otherwise. Minimum cover is what we Americans call Free of Particular Average (FPA) and most others call Institute Cargo Clauses C. Either way, this coverage is extremely limited, and the parties should consider providing for additional risks for most shipments. **For the first time, such additional coverage is mentioned as an option in A3 of CIP. Also, specific Institute Cargo Clauses are mentioned.**

BUYER-SELLER RESPONSIBILITIES

The following is a short list of responsibilities.

1. **Goods and Payment**
   The seller must ship the goods when promised, and must promptly notify the buyer that they have done so. The buyer must pay the seller. Since the seller is arranging transport, it should be aware of what packaging is needed. **However, the packaging definition found in <u>Incoterms® 2010</u> states that these rules do not cover container stowage and that this should be covered elsewhere in the sales contract. This is new.**
2. **Loading and unloading**
   The seller is responsible for loading, and the buyer is responsible for unloading.
3. **Pre-carriage and main carriage (and on-carriage?)**
   The seller is responsible for payment of carriage to the agreed place. However, the default position is that the seller delivers by handing over the goods to the first carrier, which could cause problems unless carriage is contracted on a "door-to-somewhere" basis
4. **Export clearance**
   This is a seller responsibility under this rule.
5. **Other hoops and hurdles**

The parties must work together on cargo security information. This usually means one party telling the other what is required and the other party providing it. Since security regulations change often and vary from country to country and from one transport mode to another, Incoterms® rules are limited to making the parties aware that they must be addressed. This is covered in A10-B10.

6. **Insurance**
   The seller is required to provide at least minimum cover insurance under CIP. Additional coverage should be considered.
7. **Documentary implications**
   a. Commercial Documents: The seller should provide a commercial invoice, a packing list, and any other commercial documents cited in the sales contract.
   b. Transport Documents: The seller must provide a freight-prepaid transport document if requested by the buyer.
   c. Insurance Document: The seller should provide proof of insurance permitting the buyer or others with insurable interest to claim directly on the insurer. For domestic use, the parties may consider alternative claiming procedures.
   d. Export Control Documentation: The seller is obligated to handle export clearance under both CIP and the Foreign Trade Regulations. With the possible exception of specific export licenses, there is no longer a paper document involved as U.S. export reporting is done electronically.
   e. Import Entry Documentation: This is a buyer obligation. However, A10 requires the seller to provide assistance at the buyer's request, risk and cost.
8. **Payment terms considerations**
   By definition, the seller must arrange and pay for carriage to the agreed place. This means the seller is in a position to require the forwarder and carrier to provide transport documentation to its specifications, and will have access to them for use in both letters of credit and documentary collections. The fact that the seller is also arranging insurance should provide additional comfort.

STORY LINE

Otto and Andre

Otto is a young importer of widgets located in Baden Baden, Germany. Andre is Otto's French widget supplier, located in Strasbourg, France, quite near the German border. Andre has blanket inland marine coverage which automatically attaches to his shipments. The cost is already factored in his selling prices.

Otto and Glotz

As we saw in Chapter 7, Otto wishes to purchase from Glotz Industries, a Fort Wayne widget manufacturer. Both are literally starting from scratch. After Otto rejected Glotz's EXW proposal, Glotz requoted using FCA. Otto requested another quotation on a freight-paid basis for comparison, to which Glotz added Institute Clauses A marine insurance at an attractive premium. They also obtained an attractive airport-to-door freight quotation enabling them to include the cost of on-carriage to Otto's premises. See proforma invoice 11.1

Gordie and Glotz
This parallels Otto and Andre above.

Riddle and Glotz
Riddle always gets lower freight costs, and never purchases on a freight-prepaid basis.

AMERICAN VIEWPOINT

The best standard coverage is Institute Cargo Clauses A (LMA/IUA) or its equivalent. This is what we Americans mistakenly call "All Risks" (and really should call "Almost All Risks"). Whatever name you use, it should be enhanced by Strike, Riot and Civil Commotion coverage and War coverage. You may also want to consider having it written on a Warehouse to Warehouse basis, which is the insurance jargon equivalent for door-to-door. Note: The Institute Clauses were revised in 2009. Check what is and isn't included in these newly drafted clauses or their equivalent coverages with your insurer.

The unloading logic is the same as found in FCA + location other than seller's premises, as the buyer is normally better positioned to unload than is the remote seller.

International use
This Incoterms® rule tasks the seller with export clearance. For U.S. exporters, this is consistent with the Foreign Trade Regulations. The seller, known as the United States Principal Party in Interest (USPPI), is required to file the EEI or appoint an agent to do so, usually a seller-appointed forwarder. As the USPPI is contracting for transportation, it will have the necessary transportation information to file.

Delivery at the first carrier can cause problems for inexperienced users when pre-carriage is contracted independently of main carriage. Here's an extreme example. A "mom & pop" truck line was transporting an expensive yacht to a seaport for shipment against a port-to-port contract of main carriage. The truck crashed on the Indiana Toll Road and never reached the port. Sadly, mom, pop, the truck and the yacht are no more. Upon whom does the foreign buyer claim? Under CIP, the answer can be the insurance company, provided the coverage is adequate and correctly written.

Since both the carrier and presumably the forwarder are working for the seller, there should be no problem obtaining documents necessary to make payment terms work. However, don't be surprised to receive letters of credit calling for "on board ocean bills of lading," extending the beneficiary's risk through vessel loading. Many banks simply will not accept a "received for shipment" document, regardless of the fact that this agrees with the seller's CIP Incoterms® obligation. Others confuse the "on board-ness" with consignment instructions. It is perfectly possible to have a negotiable received for shipment marine transportation document. Fortunately, as the seller is contracting for main carriage, it is not unreasonable that it be responsible for the carrier's loading obligations.

Another seller advantage is that each shipment made under C-Group Incoterms® rules is another that is counted to its credit in negotiating shippers' agreements. Since the seller is the party contracting for transportation with the carrier, it is the shipper. Service providers respect VOLUME above all. Shippers that control many shipments have, do, and always will pay lower freight costs and get better service than less frequent shippers.

Experienced U.S. importers may prefer to buy on an F-Group term unless their suppliers offer exceptionally attractive freight costs. If this is the case, consider holding the seller responsible for the carrier it chooses by requesting DAT or DAP rather than C-Group rules. These rules also take the "first carrier" situation off the table. In any case, insist on proof of what the freight costs are such as a rated transport document to avoid paying import duty on inbound freight costs.

Depending on the stature of the buyer's insurance company and the currency of the contract, CIP buyers may want to consider obtaining contingency insurance. This is coverage issued by one insurer against the possibility of default by another.

Domestic use

Except for buyers attempting to achieve large shipper status, CIP presents no problem for purely domestic transactions.

CIP does present a minor issue for domestic use, as most coverage for domestic shipments is written under what is called inland marine coverage. Unlike marine cargo insurance used for international shipments, inland marine is normally written to automatically cover all domestic shipments over an agreed period for a fixed premium. The policy holder normally claims in case of damage or loss. However, the CIP Incoterms® rule specifies that the buyer or other parties with insurable interest must be able to claim directly from the insurer. This can usually be addressed by a seller commitment to file any necessary claims in the buyer's behalf.

[xxv] Incoterms® 2010 (ISBN 978-92-842-0080-1), ICC No. 720, ICC Publishing SA, Paris, France, available from ICC Publishing Inc., New York, NY

PROFORMA INVOICE

EXPORTER Glotz Industries Inc 1492 Columbus Boulevard Fort Wayne, Indiana 12345-6789 USA	**PROFORMA INVOICE #** 11.1 **PROFORMA INVOICE DATE** October 20, 2010 **PROFORMA VALIDITY DATE** November 20, 2010 **EST'D SHIPMENT DATE** November 11, 2010
SOLD TO Widgets by Otto III Dean Haberkampstrasse Baden Baden GERMANY	**TERMS OF PAYMENT** Net 30 days **SHIPMENT/DELIVERY TERMS** CIP Dean Haberkampstrasse, Baden Baden, Germany, Incoterms 2010
SHIP TO Same as SOLD TO	**TITLE** Ownership transfers when payment is received by seller

QUANTITY	UNITS	DESCRIPTION OF MERCHANDISE	UNIT PRICE	TOTAL
20	Each	Blue widgets	100.00	2000.00

LAW & DISPUTE RESOLUTION: The U.N. Convention on Contracts for the International Sale of Goods (1980) shall apply to this offer and any resulting contract. Any disputes will be resolved by binding arbitration services of the International Chamber of Commerce.	**MERCHANDISE TOTAL** Export Packing Pre-carriage Main carriage and on-carriage Insurance (A+ War & Strike) (warehouse-warehouse) Forwarding	**US$** 2000.00 123.00 138.00 630.00 24.41 100.00
	GRAND TOTAL CIP Baden Baden	**US$** 3015.41

Chapter 12 - Delivered At Terminal

Abbreviation: DAT
Transport mode: all
Contract type: arrival
Place: a terminal on the buyer's side of transportation

Delivered At Terminal is a new Incoterms® rule designed to broaden the old Delivered Ex Quay (DEQ). Unlike its predecessor, DAT can be used with any mode of transportation and either single carrier or multimodal. The place must be at a terminal on the buyer's side of the transportation for which the seller contracts. Possibilities include a quay next to an arriving vessel at an arrival port (like DEQ), or an airport, a truck terminal, a container yard, etc. Since this is where the seller's risk and cost end, it should be spelled out in as much detail as possible as many ports and airports are huge.

Unlike the other Incoterms® 2010 rules, DAT sellers are responsible for unloading the contract goods. Sellers should carefully contract for transportation to match the agreed point at the agreed place, since buyers are not required to reimburse them for any additional costs beyond that point. This omnimodal rule is so versatile that no destination place can be set as a default. For instance, with vessel shipments, unloading can involve terminal handling and other such costs which may not apply to other transport modes like air freight. Since there is no consistency as to how and to whom carriers levy these charges, the parties should address this in their sales contract and sellers should contract for transportation accordingly.

This term is used in arrival contracts, where the parties agree that the seller delivers when the contract goods arrive at the agreed place at the agreed terminal.

Since the seller is contracting for carriage, it usually also appoints the forwarder for international transactions. This enables the seller to provide instructions to these parties without the risk of their following any conflicting instructions from the buyer.

BUYER-SELLER RESPONSIBILITIES

The following is a short list of responsibilities.

1. **Goods and Payment**
   The seller must ship the goods so as to arrive when promised, and must promptly notify the buyer that they have done so. The buyer must pay the seller. Since the seller is arranging transport, it should be aware of what packaging is needed. **However, the packaging definition found in <u>Incoterms® 2010</u>[xxvi] states that these rules do not cover container stowage and that this should be covered elsewhere in the sales contract. This is new.**

2. **Loading and unloading**
   The seller is responsible for loading, and for unloading at the destination terminal.
3. **Pre-carriage and main carriage**
   The seller is responsible for payment of carriage to the agreed terminal on the buyer's side.
4. **Export clearance**
   This is a seller responsibility under this rule.
5. **Other hoops and hurdles**
   The parties must work together on cargo security information. This usually means one party telling the other what is required and the other party providing it. Since security regulations change often and vary from country to country and from one transport mode to another, Incoterms® rules are limited to making the parties aware that they must be addressed. This is covered in A10-B10.
6. **Insurance**
   Neither party is required to insure under DAT. However, common sense dictates otherwise, and the seller should consider insurance outside of the rule because it bears the risk of loss until delivery happens at the agreed arrival terminal.
7. **Documentary implications**
   a. Commercial Documents: The seller should provide a commercial invoice, a packing list, and any other commercial documents cited in the sales contract.
   b. Transport Documents: The seller must provide a document enabling the buyer to collect the goods at the terminal. While this could be a freight-prepaid transport document, it would be strictly speaking insufficient as it indicates only that shipment has been made, not that it has successfully arrived.
   c. Export Control Documentation: The seller is obligated to handle export clearance under both DAT and the Foreign Trade Regulations. With the possible exception of specific export licenses, there is no longer a paper document involved as U.S. export reporting is done electronically.
   d. Import Entry Documentation: This is a buyer obligation. However, A10 requires the seller to provide assistance at the buyer's request, risk and cost.
8. **Payment terms considerations**
   By definition, the seller must arrange and pay for carriage to the agreed place. It is in a position to require the forwarder and carrier to provide transport documentation to its specifications. While the parties may agree to a freight-paid transport document for documentary collections and letters of credit, this does not conclusively prove that the goods have arrived. On the other hand, a document issued on arrival at the terminal would often be too late for use with letters of credit and documentary collections.

STORY LINE

Otto and Andre

Otto is a young importer of widgets located in Baden Baden, Germany. Andre is Otto's French widget supplier, located in Strasbourg, France, quite near the German border. They never use this rule as the places are served by carriers providing door-to-door transportation, and Otto sometimes picks up his orders himself.

Otto and Glotz
As we saw in Chapter 7, Otto wishes to purchase from Glotz Industries, a Fort Wayne widget manufacturer. Both are literally starting from scratch. Having already quoted a price to Otto's premises in Chapter 11, Glotz would not be accomplishing anything by quoting DAT Frankfurt airport.

Gordie and Glotz
Gordie has a warehouse that supplies a gold mining operation in a remote part of the Yukon territory where there is no common carrier service. Glotz ships to the truck line terminal in Whitehorse, and Gordie's warehouse manager picks the shipment up there. See proforma 12.1

Jerry and Glotz
They could have used DAT Laredo but decided to continue using FCA Laredo. For both rules, Glotz would deliver when the goods arrive at Laredo and would pay the freight cost to get them there. However, unloading is done by Jerry's forwarder, not Glotz's carrier.

Riddle and Glotz
Riddle always gets lower freight costs, and never purchases on a freight-prepaid basis.

AMERICAN VIEWPOINT

International use
This new Incoterms® 2010 rule is used in arrival contracts where the seller delivers by unloading at an agreed destination terminal and is the only rule that specifically tasks the seller with unloading.

It works well with "somewhere-to-terminal (port, airport, ground)" transportation contracts that include unloading. However, the parties must take care that the buyer isn't also charged with associated costs which were covered in the prepaid transportation contract provided by the seller. This requires constant attention as there is no consistency in the way such costs are charged.

Another use for this term is for break-bulk shipments on geared vessels to small ports, jobsites, etc. where the unloading is handled by the vessel itself. A third is for shipment to places that are not served by common carriers, as in our Gordie example.

As with all D-Group rules, DAT tasks the seller with export clearance which for U.S. exporters is consistent with the Foreign Trade Regulations. The seller, known as the United States Principal Party in Interest (USPPI), is required to file the EEI or appoint an agent to do so, usually a seller-appointed forwarder. As the USPPI is contracting for transportation, it will have the necessary transportation information to file.

Another seller advantage is that each shipment made under D-Group Incoterms® rules is another that is counted to its credit in negotiating shippers' agreements. Since the seller is the party contracting for transportation with the carrier, it is the shipper. Service providers respect VOLUME above all. Shippers that control many shipments have, do, and always will pay lower freight costs and get better service than less frequent shippers.

Publicly traded corporations will find that the arrival nature of this rule can result in delayed revenue recognition, and may prefer to use C-Group rules.

Experienced U.S. importers may prefer to buy on an F-Group term unless their suppliers offer exceptionally attractive freight costs. In any case, insist on proof of what the freight costs are such as a rated transport document to avoid paying import duty on inbound freight costs.

Domestic use

This plays out the same as international use except for export clearance.

[xxvi] Incoterms®2010, (ISBN 978-92-842-0080-1), ICC No. 720, ICC Publishing SA, Paris, France, available from ICC Publishing Inc., New York, NY

PROFORMA INVOICE

EXPORTER Glotz Industries Inc 1492 Columbus Boulevard Fort Wayne, Indiana 12345-6789 USA	**PROFORMA INVOICE #** 12.1 **PROFORMA INVOICE DATE** November 8, 2010 **PROFORMA VALIDITY DATE** December 8, 2010 **EST'D SHIPMENT DATE** November 20, 2010
SOLD TO Gordie's Good Widgets 1 Carl Crewson Street North Bay, Ontario CANADA	**TERMS OF PAYMENT** Net 30 days **SHIPMENT/DELIVERY TERMS** DAT Ajax Freight Terminal, Whitehorse, Canada, Incoterms 2010
SHIP TO Gordie's Good Widgets c/o Ajax Freight Whitehorse, Yukon CANADA	**TITLE** Ownership transfers when payment is received by seller

QUANTITY	UNITS	DESCRIPTION OF MERCHANDISE	UNIT PRICE	TOTAL
40	Each	Blue widgets	100.00	4000.00

LAW & DISPUTE RESOLUTION: The U.N. Convention on Contracts for the International Sale of Goods (1980) shall apply to this offer and any resulting contract. Any disputes will be resolved by binding arbitration services of the International Chamber of Commerce.	**MERCHANDISE TOTAL** Freight	**US$** 4000.00 1136.00
	GRAND TOTAL DAT Whitehorse	**US$** 5136.00

Chapter 13 - Delivered At Place

Abbreviation: DAP
Transport mode: all
Contract type: arrival
Place: an agreed place on the buyer's side of transportation

Delivered At Place is a new Incoterms® rule designed to replace the old Delivered At Frontier (DAF), Delivered Ex Ship (DES) and Delivered Duty Unpaid (DDU). DAP can be used with any mode of transportation and either single carrier or multimodal. The place must be on the buyer's side of the transportation for which the seller contracts. Possibilities include an arrival point, the buyer's premises, or anywhere else the parties agree as long as it is on the buyer's side. Since this is where the seller's risk and cost end, it should be spelled out in as much detail as possible.

Sellers should carefully contract for transportation to match the agreed point at the agreed place, since buyers are not required to reimburse them for any additional costs beyond that point. This omnimodal rule is so versatile that no destination place can be set as a default. The parties should address this in their sales contract and sellers should contract for transportation accordingly.

This term is used in arrival contracts, where the parties agree that the seller delivers when the contract goods arrive at the agreed place.

Since the seller is contracting for carriage, it usually also appoints the forwarder for international transactions. This enables the seller to provide instructions to these parties without the risk of their following any conflicting instructions from the buyer.

BUYER-SELLER RESPONSIBILITIES

The following is a short list of responsibilities.

1. **Goods and Payment**
   The seller must ship the goods so as to arrive when promised, and must promptly notify the buyer that they have done so. The buyer must pay the seller. Since the seller is arranging transport, it should be aware of what packaging is needed. **However, the packaging definition found in <u>Incoterms® 2010</u>[xxvii] states that these rules do not cover container stowage and that this should be covered elsewhere in the sales contract. This is new.**
2. **Loading and unloading**
   The seller is responsible for loading, and the buyer is responsible for unloading.

3. **Pre-carriage and main carriage (and on-carriage?)**
   The seller is responsible for payment of carriage to the agreed place on the buyer's side.
4. **Export clearance**
   This is a seller responsibility under this rule.
5. **Other hoops and hurdles**
   The parties must work together on cargo security information. This usually means one party telling the other what is required and the other party providing it. Since security regulations change often and vary from country to country and from one transport mode to another, Incoterms® rules are limited to making the parties aware that they must be addressed. This is covered in A10-B10.
6. **Insurance**
   Neither party is required to insure under DAP. However, common sense dictates otherwise, and the seller should consider insurance outside of the rule because it bears the risk of loss until delivery happens at the agreed place.
7. **Documentary implications**
   a. Commercial Documents: The seller should provide a commercial invoice, a packing list, and any other commercial documents cited in the sales contract.
   b. Transport Documents: The seller must provide a document enabling the buyer to receive the goods. While this could be a freight-prepaid transport document, it would be strictly speaking insufficient as it indicates only that shipment has been made, not that it has successfully arrived.
   c. Export Control Documentation: The seller is obligated to handle export clearance under both DAP and the Foreign Trade Regulations. With the possible exception of specific export licenses, there is no longer a paper document involved as U.S. export reporting is done electronically.
   d. Import Entry Documentation: This is a buyer obligation. However, A10 requires the seller to provide assistance at the buyer's request, risk and cost.
8. **Payment terms considerations**
   By definition, the seller must arrange and pay for carriage to the agreed place. It is in a position to require the forwarder and carrier to provide transport documentation to its specifications. While the parties may agree to a freight-paid transport document for documentary collections and letters of credit, this does not conclusively prove that the goods have arrived. On the other hand, a document issued on arrival would often be too late for use with letters of credit or documentary collections.

STORY LINE

Otto and Andre

Otto is a young importer of widgets located in Baden Baden, Germany. Andre is Otto's French widget supplier, located in Strasbourg, France, quite near the German border. Although Otto has negotiated very good freight rates with a truck line serving Strasbourg and Baden Baden, Andre has an even better rate with a small package carrier which they use for very small shipments and next-day service, and is willing to remain responsible for the condition of the goods until they arrive. See proforma 13.1.

Otto and Glotz
As we saw in Chapter 7, Otto wishes to purchase from Glotz Industries, a Fort Wayne widget manufacturer. Both are literally starting from scratch. In an attempt to obtain at least a small first order and hopefully renew the old relationship, Glotz quoted DAP Otto's premises in Baden Baden . They have listed insurance as a separate line item. See proforma 13.2

Gordie and Glotz
Glotz has negotiated exceptionally low door-to-door freight costs with a carrier that provides service to Canada. Since there is no greater risk to the cargo in Canadian transit than here, and as shipments to Canada are automatically covered under their inland marine policy, Glotz is willing to remain responsible for the condition of the goods through delivery. Since it is a privately held company, there is no pressure to recognize revenue at the earliest possible moment. See proforma 13.3.

Jerry and Glotz
Glotz is not at all comfortable remaining responsible for the condition of the goods during transit within Mexico.

Riddle and Glotz
Riddle always gets lower freight costs, and never purchases on a freight-prepaid basis.

AMERICAN VIEWPOINT

This new Incoterms® 2010 rule is used in arrival contracts where the seller delivers when the goods arrive at the agreed place on the buyer's side ready for unloading. The unloading logic is the same as found in FCA + location other than seller's premises, as the buyer is normally better positioned to unload than is the remote seller.

DAP may be used in place of the old DAF when the place is a border location, and in place of the old DES when the place is on an arriving vessel. It may also be used in place of the old and very popular DDU. In fact, besides replacing three old terms, the main reason for replacing DDU with DAP was the phrase "Duty Unpaid." See the following Domestic Use section.

Publicly traded corporations will find that the arrival nature of this rule can result in delayed revenue recognition, and may prefer to use C-Group rules.

International use
As with all D-Group rules, DAP tasks the seller with export clearance which for U.S. exporters is consistent with the Foreign Trade Regulations. The seller, known as the United States Principal Party in Interest (USPPI), is required to file the EEI or appoint an agent to do so, usually a seller-appointed forwarder. As the USPPI is contracting for transportation, it will have the necessary transportation information to file.

Another seller advantage is that each shipment made under D-Group Incoterms® rules is another that is counted to its credit in negotiating shippers' agreements. Since the seller is the party contracting for transportation with the carrier, it is the shipper. Service providers respect VOLUME above all. Shippers that control many shipments have, do, and always will pay lower freight costs and get better service than less frequent shippers.

Experienced U.S. importers may prefer to buy on an F-Group term unless their suppliers offer exceptionally attractive freight costs. In any case, insist on proof of what the freight costs are such as a rated transport document to avoid paying import duty on inbound freight costs.

Domestic use

While the default position of DAP is that the seller is not responsible for any applicable duty, the name of the term is "duty neutral." This easily lends itself to domestic sales of pre-imported, pre-cleared goods on which any applicable duty has already been paid and presumably included in the price of the goods themselves. Formerly, the most accurate term for such situations was Delivered Duty Paid. While this was fine for purely domestic transactions, its possible misuse in international situations argues for keeping it away from domestic parties who are unfamiliar with the way Incoterms® rules work. Increased domestic use here and within the EU made the need for this change very obvious.

This plays out the same as international use except for export clearance. It works well with the door-to-door ground transportation so prevalent here.

[xxvii] Incoterms®2010, (ISBN 978-92-842-0080-1), ICC No. 720, ICC Publishing SA, Paris, France, available from ICC Publishing Inc., New York, NY

PROFORMA INVOICE

EXPORTER Les Widgets de France Rue John-Pierre Robin 12 Strasbourg FRANCE	**PROFORMA INVOICE #** 13.1 **PROFORMA INVOICE DATE** November 8, 2010 **PROFORMA VALIDITY DATE** December 10, 2010 **EST'D SHIPMENT DATE** November 9, 2010
SOLD TO Widgets by Otto III Dean Haberkampstrasse Baden Baden GERMANY	**TERMS OF PAYMENT** Net 30 days **SHIPMENT/DELIVERY TERMS** DAP Dean Haberkampstrasse, Baden Baden, Germany, Incoterms 2010
SHIP TO Same as SOLD TO	**TITLE** Ownership transfers when payment is received by seller

QUANTITY	**UNITS**	**DESCRIPTION OF MERCHANDISE**	**UNIT PRICE**	**TOTAL**
2	Each	Bleu widgets	€ 100.00	200.00

LAW & DISPUTE RESOLUTION: The U.N. Convention on Contracts for the International Sale of Goods (1980) shall apply to this offer and any resulting contract. Any disputes will be resolved by binding arbitration services of the International Chamber of Commerce.	**MERCHANDISE TOTAL** Freight	€ 200.00 32.00
	GRAND TOTAL DAP Baden Baden	€ 232.00

PROFORMA INVOICE

EXPORTER
Glotz Industries Inc
1492 Columbus Boulevard
Fort Wayne, Indiana 12345-6789
USA

PROFORMA INVOICE #
13.2

PROFORMA INVOICE DATE
October 22, 2010

PROFORMA VALIDITY DATE
November 22, 2010

EST'D SHIPMENT DATE
November 15, 2010

SOLD TO
Widgets by Otto III
Dean Haberkampstrasse
Baden Baden
GERMANY

TERMS OF PAYMENT
Net 30 days

SHIPMENT/DELIVERY TERMS
DAP Dean Haberkampstrasse, Baden Baden, Germany, Incoterms 2010

SHIP TO
Same as SOLD TO

TITLE
Ownership transfers when payment is received by seller

QUANTITY	UNITS	DESCRIPTION OF MERCHANDISE	UNIT PRICE	TOTAL
20	Each	Blue widgets	100.00	2000.00

LAW & DISPUTE RESOLUTION: The U.N. Convention on Contracts for the International Sale of Goods (1980) shall apply to this offer and any resulting contract. Any disputes will be resolved by binding arbitration services of the International Chamber of Commerce.

MERCHANDISE TOTAL	**US$** 2000.00
Export Packing	123.00
Pre-carriage	138.00
Main carriage and on-carriage	630.00
Insurance (A+ War & Strike) (warehouse to warehouse)	24.41
Forwarding	100.00
GRAND TOTAL DAP Baden Baden	**US$** 3015.41

PROFORMA INVOICE

EXPORTER Glotz Industries Inc 1492 Columbus Boulevard Fort Wayne, Indiana 12345-6789 USA	**PROFORMA INVOICE #** 13.3 **PROFORMA INVOICE DATE** October 15, 2010 **PROFORMA VALIDITY DATE** November 15, 2010 **EST'D SHIPMENT DATE** October 19, 2010
SOLD TO Gordie's Good Widgets 1 Carl Crewson Street North Bay, Ontario CANADA	**TERMS OF PAYMENT** Net 30 days **SHIPMENT/DELIVERY TERMS** DAP 1 Carl Crewson Street, North Bay, Ontario, Canada, Incoterms 2010
SHIP TO Same as SOLD TO	**TITLE** Ownership transfers when payment is received by seller

QUANTITY	UNITS	DESCRIPTION OF MERCHANDISE	UNIT PRICE	TOTAL
40	Each	Blue widgets	100.00	4000.00

LAW & DISPUTE RESOLUTION: The U.N. Convention on Contracts for the International Sale of Goods (1980) shall apply to this offer and any resulting contract. Any disputes will be resolved by binding arbitration services of the International Chamber of Commerce.	**MERCHANDISE TOTAL** Freight	**US$** 4000.00 392.00
	GRAND TOTAL DAP North Bay	**US$** 4392.00

Chapter 14 - Delivered Duty Paid

Abbreviation: DDP
Transport mode: all
Contract type: arrival
Place: an agreed place on the buyer's side of transportation

Delivered Duty Paid can be used with any mode of transportation and either single carrier or multimodal. The place must be on the buyer's side of the transportation for which the seller contracts. Possibilities include an arrival point, the buyer's premises, or anywhere else the parties agree as long as it is on the buyer's side. Since this is where the seller's risk and cost end, it should be spelled out in as much detail as possible.

Sellers should carefully contract for transportation to match the agreed point at the agreed place, since buyers are not required to reimburse them for any additional costs beyond that point. This omnimodal rule is so versatile that no destination place can be set as a default. The parties should address this in their sales contract and sellers should contract for transportation accordingly.

This term is used in arrival contracts, where the parties agree that the seller delivers when the contract goods arrive at the agreed place. It requires the seller to handle and pay for import clearance, and as such represents the maximum seller obligation. Any applicable value added taxes are also for the seller's account unless the parties agree otherwise. This seems counterintuitive. VAT is sometimes refundable under certain circumstances, and buyers would more likely be aware of how this works in their own countries.

Since the seller is contracting for carriage, it usually also appoints the forwarder for international transactions. This enables the seller to provide instructions to these parties without the risk of their following any conflicting instructions from the buyer. As the seller is also responsible for import clearance, it will normally engage a customs broker in the buyer's country.

BUYER-SELLER RESPONSIBILITIES

The following is a short list of responsibilities.

1. **Goods and Payment**
   The seller must ship the goods so as to arrive when promised, and must promptly notify the buyer that they have done so. The buyer must pay the seller. Since the seller is arranging transport, it should be aware of what packaging is needed. **However, the packaging definition found in <u>Incoterms® 2010</u>[xxviii] states that these rules do not cover container stowage**

and that this should be covered elsewhere in the sales contract. This is new.

2. **Loading and unloading**
   The seller is responsible for loading, and the buyer is responsible for unloading.
3. **Pre-carriage and main carriage (and on-carriage?)**
   The seller is responsible for payment of carriage to the agreed place on the buyer's side.
4. **Export clearance and import clearance**
   Both are seller responsibilities under this rule.
5. **Other hoops and hurdles**
   The parties must work together on cargo security information. This usually means one party telling the other what is required and the other party providing it. Since security regulations change often and vary from country to country and from one transport mode to another, Incoterms® rules are limited to making the parties aware that they must be addressed. This is covered in A10-B10.
6. **Insurance**
   Neither party is required to insure under DDP. However, common sense dictates otherwise, and the seller should consider insurance outside of the rule because it bears the risk of loss until delivery happens at the agreed place.
7. **Documentary implications**
   a. Commercial Documents: The seller should provide a commercial invoice, a packing list, and any other commercial documents cited in the sales contract.
   b. Transport Documents: The seller must provide a document enabling the buyer to receive the goods. While this could be a freight-prepaid transport document, it would be strictly speaking insufficient as it indicates only that shipment has been made, not that it has successfully arrived.
   c. Export Control Documentation: The seller is obligated to handle export clearance under both DDP and the Foreign Trade Regulations. With the possible exception of specific export licenses, there is no longer a paper document involved as U.S. export reporting is done electronically.
   d. Import Entry Documentation: As this is a seller obligation, the seller should provide the buyer with evidence of import clearance and duty payment. However, B2 requires the buyer to provide assistance at the seller's request, risk and cost.
8. **Payment terms considerations**
   By definition, the seller must arrange and pay for carriage to the agreed place and handle import clearance. It is in a position to require the forwarder and carrier to provide transport documentation to its specifications. While the parties may agree to a freight-paid transport document for documentary collections and letters of credit, this does not conclusively prove that the goods have arrived or that they have been cleared for import. On the other hand, a document issued on arrival indicating import clearance would often be too late for use with letters of credit or documentary collections. Further, as the goods would have already entered the commerce of the buyer's country, the seller's chances of reclaiming them are slim to none. For these reasons, DDP is best suited to payment with order, open account, or standby credit terms.

STORY LINE

Otto and Andre
Otto is a young importer of widgets located in Baden Baden, Germany. As they are both in the European Union, DAP and DDP are about the same except for the VAT. As this is best handled by Otto, they do not use this rule.

Otto and Glotz
Glotz's third shipment was an unmitigated disaster. The widgets looked fine, but didn't work. This was discovered only after Otto's best customer began to use them in its manufacturing process. The result is that an entire production line is down and, German labor law being what it is, the workers continue receiving their full pay. Being a responsible supplier, Glotz is willing to move heaven and earth to make things as right as they can. They come close to doing exactly that by shipping replacements at no charge. Rather than further inconveniencing Otto, they used DDP and sent Otto the No Charge Invoice 14.1.

Gordie and Glotz
Being of sound mind, the parties have agreed that just because it is possible to be a "non-resident-importer" is no reason that this should be done.

Jerry and Glotz
No way would Glotz become involved in Mexican import clearance, even if they could.

Riddle and Glotz
Not applicable.

AMERICAN VIEWPOINT

International use
This Incoterms® 2010 rule is little changed from its 2000 predecessor, and continues to make as little sense for Americans. It is used in arrival contracts where the seller delivers when the goods arrive at the agreed place on the buyer's side, import cleared and ready for unloading. The unloading logic is the same as found in FCA + location other than seller's premises, in that the buyer is normally better positioned to unload than is the remote seller.

As with all D-Group rules, DDP tasks the seller with export clearance which for U.S. exporters is consistent with the Foreign Trade Regulations. The seller, known as the United States Principal Party in Interest (USPPI), is required to file the EEI or appoint an agent to do so, usually a seller-appointed forwarder. As the USPPI is contracting for transportation, it will have the necessary transportation information to file.

Alone among Incoterms® rules, DDP also tasks the seller with import clearance. This writer remains unconvinced that the seller is ever better positioned to deal with the buyer's country than the buyer is. Readers who consider exporting under this term may want to answer the following questions:

1. Are you sure you know how this is done in the buyer's country?

2. Are you sure you know the correct duty rate, and can it change?
3. Do you know how to select a customs broker in the buyer's country, and how much they charge?
4. Does the buyer's government permit foreign sellers to be involved in import clearance?
5. Could you unwittingly be party to Foreign Corrupt Practices Act violations if the broker acts inappropriately vis-à-vis local government officials?
6. Does the buyer's government want to deal with you?
7. Will your transactions stand out and invite above normal scrutiny?
8. How would you arrange the return of unwanted or unpaid product that has already been import cleared?

Each shipment made under D-Group Incoterms® rules is another that is counted to its credit in negotiating shippers' agreements. Since the seller is the party contracting for transportation with the carrier, it is the shipper. Service providers respect VOLUME above all. Shippers that control many shipments have, do, and always will pay lower freight costs and get better service than less frequent shippers. However, this can be accomplished by more seller-friendly Incoterms® rules.

Publicly traded corporations will find that the arrival nature of this rule can result in delayed revenue recognition, and may prefer to use C-Group rules. The accountants will also just love any contingent liability remaining until DDP shipments are liquidated in the buyers' countries.

Experienced U.S. importers may prefer to buy on an F-Group term unless their suppliers offer exceptionally attractive freight costs. Even then, they should opt for DAP rather than DDP. Reasons include:

1. Any sane overseas seller will be as concerned about U.S. import clearance as we would be about theirs. There will very likely be a premium buried in the price for potential risk.
2. Compliance will depend on the competence of a Customs broker appointed by a foreign supplier.
3. Occasionally, Customs will have a routine question which the buyer could readily answer if it were the importer of record. However, with DDP, the buyer is not a party to import clearance.
4. Any drawback claims would be needlessly complicated, and would require cooperation of the foreign seller.

Domestic use

While DDP may lend itself to domestic sales of pre-imported, pre-cleared goods on which any applicable duty has already been paid and presumably included in the price of the goods themselves, DAP is a better choice. The possible misuse of DDP in international situations argues for keeping it away from domestic parties who are unfamiliar with the way Incoterms® rules work. This is the reason the new DAP Incoterms® rule is so important to U.S. domestic users.

[xxviii] Incoterms®2010, (ISBN 978-92-842-0080-1), ICC No. 720, ICC Publishing SA, Paris, France, available from ICC Publishing Inc., New York, NY

NO CHARGE INVOICE

EXPORTER Glotz Industries Inc 1492 Columbus Boulevard Fort Wayne, Indiana 12345-6789 USA	**INVOICE #** 14.1 **INVOICE DATE** January 3, 2011 **EST'D SHIPMENT DATE** January 3, 2011
SOLD TO Widgets by Otto III Dean Haberkampstrasse Baden Baden GERMANY	**TERMS OF PAYMENT** No Charge – Value for Customs purposes only **SHIPMENT/DELIVERY TERMS** DDP Dean Haberkampstrasse, Baden Baden, Germany, Incoterms 2010
SHIP TO Same as SOLD TO	**TITLE** Ownership transfers when payment is received by seller

QUANTITY	**UNITS**	**DESCRIPTION OF MERCHANDISE**	**UNIT PRICE**	**TOTAL**
20	Each	Blue widgets	100.00	2000.00

LAW & DISPUTE RESOLUTION: The U.N. Convention on Contracts for the International Sale of Goods (1980) shall apply to this offer and any resulting contract. Any disputes will be resolved by binding arbitration services of the International Chamber of Commerce.	**MERCHANDISE TOTAL** Export Packing Pre-carriage Main carriage and on-carriage Insurance (A+ War & Strike) (warehouse to warehouse) Forwarding Import Clearance	**US$** 2000.00 123.00 138.00 630.00 24.41 100.00 350.00
	GRAND TOTAL DDP Baden Baden	**US$** 3365.41

Chapter 15 - Free Alongside Ship

Abbreviation: FAS
Transport mode: vessel only
Contract type: shipment
Place: next to a buyer-appointed vessel at the agreed port on the seller's side

Free Alongside Ship (FAS) is a venerable marine-only Incoterms® rule. Its practical use is generally limited to non-containerized waterborne shipments where the buyer contracts not only for main carriage but for vessel loading as well.

A3 of the FAS rule states that the seller is not tasked with providing carriage. However, the place is next to a buyer-appointed vessel, and the seller must get the goods there in order to deliver. The "no carriage" refers to main carriage here, as well as with the FCA + other location on seller's side and FOB Incoterms® 2010 rules.

FAS reflects the way most cargo was handled prior to containerization. Ports were little more than collections of piers to which outbound cargo was delivered. Nowadays, most modern ports are very secure areas. Outbound cargo is normally handed over some distance from the ships, and this is particularly true for containerized transportation. Still, there are instances where FAS is appropriate:

- with vessel chartering, where the buyer handles loading and main carriage, as is common in commodity trades or with break-bulk shipments of project cargo,
- where port rules define "along side" to be somewhere other than directly next to a vessel,
- with lighterage, where ships are loaded from smaller vessels rather from piers,
- with containers at small or less developed ports and vessels with loading capability,
- when the goods have been sold after delivery alongside the ship.

It has probably occurred to you that FCA + the appropriate place could be substituted for every one of these situations. You may also have noticed that the 2010 revision brings a major shift toward omnimodal rules. Maybe next time.

The FAS rule is used for shipment contracts as the seller delivers when the goods arrive at the agreed place at the agreed port within time frame agreed by the parties.

The seller must also notify the buyer either that the goods have been delivered or that the buyer-appointed carrier failed to receive them.

The location within the port should be described in geographic terms in as much detail as possible. With charter vessels, timing is extremely important because of the huge costs of needlessly tying up an entire vessel. Conversely, there are significant costs and risks in having goods arrive prematurely at a port awaiting the vessel. Sellers, buyers and carriers should work closely to coordinate the ship's arrival and the delivery of the goods.

International shipments are accommodated since sellers are responsible for export clearance. Exporters need to exercise due diligence as they are not in a position to know the disposition of their shipments once they are delivered. However, as they are bringing the goods to a buyer-appointed vessel, they are a transport leg closer to the actual export than is the case with EXW or FCA + seller's premises. Savvy U.S. exporters use the Census Bureau's FTRs to their advantage by obtaining written authorizations from their buyers to file the EEIs. They then insist that the buyer-appointed forwarders and carriers provide the transportation information in writing to enable them to do the filing. The buyers should have no reluctance to provide authorizations since under the FAS rule they have already agreed that the sellers do this. In fact, any buyer reluctance should be treated with suspicion as it would be contrary to the sales contract.

A4 of the FAS rule contains an innovation by adding a provision covering goods that have already been delivered. This is intended to facilitate the use of this rule in commodity trade, where goods are commonly sold while in transit (so called "string sales").

Note: Although arranging for any main carriage is strictly speaking a buyer obligation, sellers sometimes take on this task for the buyers at the buyers' risk and cost. The resulting documentation would be a freight-collect transport document, with carriage arrangements made by the seller for the account of the buyer. Given the fact that FAS is used often with vessel charter situations, this would be unusual.

BUYER-SELLER RESPONSIBILITIES

The following is a short list of responsibilities.

1. **Goods and Payment**
   The seller must have the goods available when promised, suitably packaged, and must transport them to the agreed place at the agreed port on the seller's side. The buyer must pay the seller. **Note: the packaging definition found in <u>Incoterms® 2010[xxix]</u> states that these rules do not cover container stowage and that this should be covered elsewhere in the sales contract. This is new.**
2. **Loading and unloading**
   The seller is responsible for unloading the delivering conveyance and placing the goods alongside the ship.
3. **Pre-carriage**
   This is a seller responsibility under this rule.
4. **Export clearance**
   This is a seller responsibility under this rule.
5. **Other hoops and hurdles**
   The parties must work together on cargo security information. This usually means one party telling the other what is required and the other party providing it. Since security regulations change often and vary from country to country and from one transport mode to another, Incoterms® rules are limited to making the parties aware that they must be addressed. This is covered in A10-B10.

6. **Insurance**
Neither party is required to insure under FAS. However, common sense dictates otherwise, and insurance should be addressed outside of the rule. Sellers bear the risk of loss until the goods are delivered next to the vessel (check with your insurers about FAS/FOB coverage). Buyers are at risk thereafter.
7. **Documentary implications**
   a. Commercial Documents: The seller should provide a commercial invoice, a packing list, and any other commercial documents cited in the sales contract.
   b. Transport Documents: The seller should provide evidence that the contract goods were delivered to the agreed place. For charter vessel shipments this could be a mate's receipt. However, for shipments made on liner terms there is no specific document. A dock receipt might do, provided it indicates that the goods were placed next to the agreed vessel at the agreed place and port within the agreed time. Same for any other "received for shipment" marine transport document. Most do not provide that level of detail. On the other hand, since the seller is not responsible for vessel loading, an "on board" document would be inappropriate.
   c. Export Control Documentation: The seller is obligated to handle export clearance. In a routed transaction, as the USPPI, the seller is obligated at a minimum to provide company and product specific information to the buyer-appointed agent for EEI filing. Proactive sellers who obtain buyer authorizations and file the EEIs will have an electronic record of filing. With the possible exception of specific export licenses, there is no longer a paper document involved as U.S. export reporting is done electronically.
   d. Import Entry Documentation: This is a buyer obligation. However, A10 requires the seller to provide assistance at the buyer's request, risk and cost.

8 **Payment terms considerations**
These transactions are frequently quite large. By definition, the seller must arrange for delivery next to the vessel. It then follows that the seller must be prepared to turn the goods over at that place. This means there's no way to use documents to restrict possession of the goods. This argues strongly for open account or payment in advance. It is possible that a mate's receipt or a sufficiently detailed dock receipt could be used to trigger a letter of credit. It is also possible that a sufficiently detailed negotiable freight collect received-for-shipment transportation document could be used both for letters of credit and documentary collections. However, as the seller is not contracting for main carriage, the risk exists that the buyer-appointed carrier or forwarder may not follow any seller-provided instructions, or may refuse to provide the needed document to the seller.

STORY LINE

None of the "usual suspects" would dream of using the FAS Incoterms® rule in day-to-day business. However, Glotz had some very large surplus equipment that was in good condition. It couldn't achieve the production economies needed for North America, but could be perfectly useful in a smaller market with lower labor costs. A Vietnamese manufacturer heard about it through a machinery broker and determined that it would suit his fledging operation. Glotz quoted a price that included disassembling the equipment and transporting it to a Great Lakes port where they were able to obtain permission to bring it pier side. See proforma 15.1. The buyer chartered space on a small tramp vessel that called on that port, and through the ship owner's agent was able to arrange for vessel loading and stowing. The parties agreed to letter of credit payable at sight against a clean dock receipt indicating shipside delivery.

AMERICAN VIEWPOINT

Quite a bit of cargo moves by chartered vessel in terms of tonnage. Bulk commodities are usually transported this way, although container imbalances have made U.S. produce exporters aware of the benefits of containerization. Huge pieces of project cargo are transported on geared vessels (those equipped with lifting capability). These shipments tend to be large and require detailed planning and execution by all parties.

International use
While the Incoterms® rule tasks the seller with export clearance, this can be at odds with local regulations.

Routed transactions: For U.S. exports, the Census Bureau's Foreign Trade Regulations require the party appointed by the buyer to file the Electronic Export Information (EEI). This usually translates to a buyer-appointed forwarder (or carrier as their roles are increasingly becoming interchangeable) . The seller, known as the United States Principal Party in Interest (USPPI), is required to provide this party with the company and product specific information necessary to file the EEI. In return, the USPPI is entitled only to written confirmation from this service provider with respect to the information it provided. The USPPI has no right to the transportation information in this situation as the EEI is confidential between the filer and Census.

As mentioned earlier and explained in more detail in Chapter 19, there is relief for exporters that prefer to file their EEIs in routed transactions rather than trusting service providers over which they have no control. An additional payoff is access to the transportation information. Savvy sellers use this to help their forwarders obtain lower freight costs and better service in order to gain control of future shipments.

There are a few other potential seller risks with all F-Group rules that stem from the buyer's contracting for main carriage with the carrier. This normally means that the buyer also appoints the forwarder. Both of these service providers would therefore follow instructions from the buyer rather than any they receive from the seller. This opens the possibility of diversion which could be illegal shipment to a prohibited party or country. More likely would be commercial diversion to a non-restricted party or country other than the destination desired by the seller. Depending on the product, doing so may not violate export regulations but could seriously compromise the seller's distribution arrangements. Also, seller access to transportation documents could present a problem, particularly with document-driven payment terms.

Speaking of payment terms, don't be surprised to receive letters of credit calling for freight collect "on board ocean bills of lading," extending the beneficiary's risk through vessel loading. Many banks simply will not accept a dock receipt or other "received for shipment" document, regardless of the fact that this agrees with the seller's FAS Incoterms® obligation. Others confuse the "on board-ness" with consignment instructions. (It is perfectly possible to have a negotiable received for shipment marine transportation document.) Unfortunately, as the buyer is contracting for main carriage, the seller who is beneficiary of such a letter of credit would be at risk for the loading operations of a carrier it did not choose and may never have chosen.

For chartering, the fact that the buyer selects the main carrier may not be so important for a purely volume consideration. Charter shipments are often negotiated individually, largely depending on vessel availability for the desired ports and times.

Experienced U.S. importers can do well with FAS. The fact that export clearance is a seller obligation makes it easier for suppliers in value added tax countries to claim refunds. Also, U.S. import duty is not payable on freight to get here, so the FAS price is usually the dutiable value. Finally, controlling the overseas forwarder really helps compliance, especially for containerized, break-bulk or Ro-Ro shipments covered by the 10+2 reporting requirements.

Domestic use

FAS presents no problem for purely domestic transactions. Barge movements come to mind, and there is growing interest in "short-sea" shipments from one U.S. port to another.

[xxix] Incoterms®2010, (ISBN 978-92-842-0080-1), ICC No. 720, ICC Publishing SA, Paris, France, available from ICC Publishing Inc., New York, NY

PROFORMA INVOICE

EXPORTER Glotz Industries Inc 1492 Columbus Boulevard Fort Wayne, Indiana 12345-6789 USA	**PROFORMA INVOICE #** 15.1 **PROFORMA INVOICE DATE** October 30, 2010 **PROFORMA VALIDITY DATE** November 30, 2010 **EST'D SHIPMENT DATE** December 5, 2010
SOLD TO Vietnam Widgets Ltd. 4 Nixon Way Ho Chi Minh City VIETNAM	**TERMS OF PAYMENT** Irrevocable, confirmed letter of credit, payable at sight **SHIPMENT/DELIVERY TERMS** FAS Port of Toledo, Ohio, USA, Incoterms 2010
SHIP TO Port of Toledo Toledo, Ohio USA	**TITLE** Ownership transfers when payment is received by seller

QUANTITY	UNITS	DESCRIPTION OF MERCHANDISE	UNIT PRICE	TOTAL
1	Each	Used, complete widget manufacturing machine serial # 718-56, tested and operating at seller's premises before disassembly and shipment	973,500.00	973,500.00

LAW & DISPUTE RESOLUTION: The U.N. Convention on Contracts for the International Sale of Goods (1980) shall apply to this offer and any resulting contract. Any disputes will be resolved by binding arbitration services of the International Chamber of Commerce.	**MERCHANDISE TOTAL** Export Packing Pre-carriage to port Terminal handling	**US$** 973500.00 7230.00 3192.00 625.00
	GRAND TOTAL FAS Port of Toledo, Ohio	**US$** 984547.00

Chapter 16 - Free On Board

Abbreviation: FOB
Transport mode: vessel only
Contract type: shipment
Place: loaded onto a buyer-appointed vessel at the agreed port on the seller's side

Free On Board (FOB) is probably the oldest shipment-delivery term, predating not only Incoterms® rules but ship lines and possibly even cargo cranes. It is widely overused, particularly in the United States. Its correct Incoterms® use should be limited to non-containerized waterborne shipments where the buyer contracts for main carriage and the seller handles vessel loading.

A3 of the FOB rule states that the seller is not tasked with providing carriage. However, the place is on board a buyer-appointed vessel, and the seller must get the goods there in order to deliver. The "no carriage" refers to main carriage here, as well as with the FCA + other location on seller's side and FAS Incoterms® 2010 rules.

The concept of "ship's rail" has been dropped from the FOB rule. Sellers deliver the goods when they are on board the buyer-appointed vessel. This is not as significant as it first appears, as A4 in both Incoterms 2000 and Incoterms® 2010 both say on board. However, removal of the "ship's rail" phrase could increase seller responsibility. As "on board" is not defined, the parties should agree on exactly what this entails, particularly for charter movements.

A4 of the FOB rule contains another innovation by adding a provision covering goods that have already been delivered. This is intended to facilitate the use of this rule in commodity trade, where goods are commonly sold while in transit (so called "string sales").

FOB reflects the way most cargo was handled prior to containerization. Ports were little more than collections of piers to which outbound cargo was delivered. Nowadays, most modern ports are very secure areas. Outbound cargo is normally handed over some distance from the ships, and this is particularly true for containerized transportation. Further, most scheduled ship lines load and unload their own vessels which they can do as they regularly call on the same ports. Still, there are instances where FOB is appropriate:

- with vessel chartering, where the seller handles vessel loading while the buyer handles main carriage, as is common in commodity trades or with break-bulk shipments of project cargo,
- other marine transport situations where the seller is better positioned to load,
- when the seller is willing to remain responsible for the loading performance of a buyer-appointed carrier,
- when the goods are sold after they have been loaded,
- with containers at small or less developed ports.

Despite the fact that its correct use is limited, it is unlikely that the FOB Incoterms® rule will be deleted for many years to come. There are simply too many legacy issues.

The FOB rule is used for shipment contracts as the seller delivers when the goods are loaded on the buyer- appointed vessel at the agreed port within the time frame agreed by the parties.

The seller must also notify the buyer either that the goods have been delivered or that the buyer-appointed carrier failed to receive them.

The location within the port should be described in geographic terms in as much detail as possible. With charter vessels, timing is extremely important because of the huge costs of needlessly tying up an entire vessel. Conversely, there are significant costs and risks in having goods arrive prematurely at a port awaiting the vessel. Sellers, buyers and carriers should work closely to coordinate the ship's arrival and the delivery of the goods.

International shipments are accommodated since sellers are responsible for export clearance. Exporters need to exercise due diligence as they are not in a position to know the disposition of their shipments once they are delivered. However, as they are putting the goods on a buyer-appointed vessel, they are a transport leg closer to the actual export than is the case with EXW or FCA + seller's premises. Savvy U.S. exporters use the Census Bureau's FTRs to their advantage by obtaining written authorizations from their buyers to file the EEIs. They then insist that the buyer-appointed forwarders and carriers provide the transportation information in writing to enable them to do the filing. The buyers should have no reluctance to provide authorizations since under the FOB rule they have already agreed that the sellers do this. In fact, any buyer reluctance should be treated with suspicion as it would be contrary to the sales contract.

Note: Although arranging for any main carriage is strictly speaking a buyer obligation, sellers sometimes take on this task for the buyers at the buyers' risk and cost. The resulting documentation would be a freight-collect transport document, with carriage arrangements made by the seller for the account of the buyer.

BUYER-SELLER RESPONSIBILITIES

The following is a short list of responsibilities.

1. **Goods and Payment**
   The seller must have the goods available when promised, suitably packaged, must transport them and load them onto the agreed vessel at the agreed port on the seller's side. The buyer must pay the seller.
   Note: the packaging definition found in <u>Incoterms® 2010</u>1 states that these rules do not cover container stowage and that this should be covered elsewhere in the sales contract. This is new.
2. **Loading and unloading**
   The seller is responsible for loading the goods onto the buyer appointed vessel.
3. **Pre-carriage**
   This is a seller responsibility under this rule.
4. **Export clearance**
   This is a seller responsibility under this rule.

5. **Other hoops and hurdles**
The parties must work together on cargo security information. This usually means one party telling the other what is required and the other party providing it. Since security regulations change often and vary from country to country and from one transport mode to another, Incoterms® rules are limited to making the parties aware that they must be addressed. This is covered in A10-B10.
6. **Insurance**
Neither party is required to insure under FOB. However, common sense dictates otherwise, and insurance should be addressed outside of the rule. Sellers bear the risk of loss until the goods are placed on board the vessel (check with your insurers about FAS/FOB coverage). Buyers are at risk thereafter.
7. **Documentary implications**
    a. Commercial Documents: The seller should provide a commercial invoice, a packing list, and any other commercial documents cited in the sales contract.
    b. Transport Documents: The seller should provide evidence that the contract goods were loaded on the vessel. This should be an "on board" freight collect marine transport document.
    c. Export Control Documentation: The seller is obligated to handle export clearance. In a routed transaction, as the USPPI, the seller is obligated at a minimum to provide company and product specific information to the buyer-appointed agent for EEI filing. Proactive sellers who obtain buyer authorizations and file the EEIs will have an electronic record of filing. With the possible exception of specific export licenses, there is no longer a paper document involved as U.S. export reporting is done electronically.
    d. Import Entry Documentation: This is a buyer obligation. However, A10 requires the seller to provide assistance at the buyer's request, risk and cost.
8. **Payment terms considerations**
By definition, the seller must arrange for loading the goods onto the vessel. The only appropriate document would be one indicating that the goods are "on board." Since the buyer is contracting for transportation, it would be freight collect. This document could easily be used to trigger payment under a letter of credit. If negotiable (consigned to "order") it can also be used for documentary collections. However, as the seller is not contracting for main carriage, the risk exists that the buyer-appointed carrier or forwarder may not follow any seller-provided instructions, or may refuse to provide the needed document to the seller.

STORY LINE

None of the "usual suspects" would dream of using the FOB Incoterms® rule in day-to-day business. However, Glotz had some very large surplus equipment that was in good condition. It couldn't achieve the production economies needed for North America, but could be perfectly useful in a smaller market with lower labor costs. A Vietnamese manufacturer heard about it through a machinery broker and determined that it would suit his fledging operation. Glotz quoted a price that included disassembling the equipment and transporting it to a Great Lakes port where they were able to obtain permission to bring it pier side. The buyer chartered space on a small tramp vessel that called on that port. However, the intended vessel was damaged en-route, and the last minute replacement did not have a large enough crane. As a concession to the buyer, Glotz agreed to handle vessel loading for an additional

$6709 to cover loading charges as shown in proforma invoice 16.1. The parties agreed to have the letter of credit amended to require a clean on board freight collect bill of lading rather than the clean dock receipt indicating shipside delivery originally required.

AMERICAN VIEWPOINT

Quite a bit of cargo moves by chartered vessel in terms of tonnage. Bulk commodities are usually transported this way, although container imbalances have made U.S. produce exporters aware of the benefits of containerization. Huge pieces of project cargo are transported by vessel. These shipments tend to be large and require detailed planning and execution by all parties. FOB works particularly well for products typically loaded by sellers from pier side facilities, such as liquids from tank farms, grain from elevators, etc.

International use
While the Incoterms® rule tasks the seller with export clearance, this can be at odds with local regulations.

Routed transactions: For U.S. exports, the Census Bureau's Foreign Trade Regulations require the party appointed by the buyer to file the Electronic Export Information (EEI). This usually translates to a buyer-appointed forwarder (or carrier as their roles are increasingly becoming interchangeable) . The seller, known as the United States Principal Party in Interest (USPPI), is required to provide this party with the company and product specific information necessary to file the EEI. In return, the USPPI is entitled only to written confirmation from this service provider with respect to the information it provided. The USPPI has no right to the transportation information in this situation as the EEI is confidential between the filer and Census.

As mentioned earlier and explained in more detail in Chapter 19, there is relief for exporters that prefer to file their EEIs in routed transactions rather than trusting service providers over which they have no control. An additional payoff is access to the transportation information. Savvy sellers use this to help <u>their</u> forwarders obtain lower freight costs and better service in order to gain control of future shipments.

There are a few other potential seller risks with all F-Group rules that stem from the buyer's contracting for main carriage with the carrier. This normally means that the buyer also appoints the forwarder. Both of these service providers would therefore follow instructions from the buyer rather than any they receive from the seller. This opens the possibility of diversion which could be illegal shipment to a prohibited party or country. More likely would be commercial diversion to a non-restricted party or country other than the destination desired by the seller. Depending on the product, doing so may not violate export regulations but could seriously compromise the seller's distribution arrangements. Also, seller access to transportation documents could present a problem, particularly with document-driven payment terms.

Bankers are quite attached to "on board ocean bills of lading."

For chartering, the fact that the buyer selects the main carrier may not be so important for a purely volume consideration. Charter shipments are often negotiated individually, largely depending on vessel availability for the desired ports and times. However, for non-charter movements VOLUME is king, and sellers seeking large shipper status are not helped by shipments on F-Group rules.

Experienced U.S. importers can do well with FOB. The fact that export clearance is a seller obligation makes it easier for suppliers in value added tax countries to claim refunds. Also, U.S. import duty is not payable on freight to get here, so the FOB price is usually the dutiable value. As we saw above, freight cost savings and superior carrier service accrue to buyers who control enough shipments to become large shippers. Finally, controlling the overseas forwarder really helps compliance, especially for containerized, break-bulk or Ro-Ro shipments covered by U.S. Government 10+2 reporting requirements.

Domestic use

Used correctly the FOB Incoterms® 2010 rule presents no problem for purely domestic transactions. Barge movements come to mind, and there is growing interest in "short-sea" shipments from one U.S. port to another.

Although deleted as obsolete from the Uniform Commercial Code in 2004, the old "FOB here, there and everywhere" shipment and delivery term remains in the law of most states and in general domestic use. It is likely that farsighted U.S. buyers and sellers will start using Incoterms® 2010 rules in domestic trade. Readers wishing to consider doing so will find a match-up from the old UCC shipment and delivery terms to Incoterms® 2010 rules in Chapter 19.

I Incoterms®2010, (ISBN 978-92-842-0080-1), ICC No. 720, ICC Publishing SA, Paris, France, available from ICC Publishing Inc., New York, NY

PROFORMA INVOICE

EXPORTER Glotz Industries Inc 1492 Columbus Boulevard Fort Wayne, Indiana 12345-6789 USA	**PROFORMA INVOICE #** 16.1 **PROFORMA INVOICE DATE** December 1, 2010 **PROFORMA VALIDITY DATE** December 31, 2010 **EST'D SHIPMENT DATE** December 15, 2010 **TERMS OF PAYMENT** Irrevocable, confirmed letter of credit, payable at sight
SOLD TO Vietnam Widgets Ltd. 4 Nixon Way Ho Chi Minh City VIETNAM	**SHIPMENT/DELIVERY TERMS** FOB Port of Toledo, Ohio, USA, Incoterms 2010
SHIP TO Port of Toledo Toledo, Ohio USA	**TITLE** Ownership transfers when payment is received by seller

QUANTITY	UNITS	DESCRIPTION OF MERCHANDISE	UNIT PRICE	TOTAL
1	Each	Used, complete widget manufacturing machine serial # 718-56, tested and operating at seller's premises before disassembly and shipment	973,500.00	973,500.00

LAW & DISPUTE RESOLUTION: The U.N. Convention on Contracts for the International Sale of Goods (1980) shall apply to this offer and any resulting contract. Any disputes will be resolved by binding arbitration services of the International Chamber of Commerce.	**MERCHANDISE TOTAL** Export Packing Pre-carriage to port Terminal handling Heavy lift & loading	**US$** 973500.00 7230.00 3192.00 625.00 6709.00
	GRAND TOTAL FOB Toledo Port, Ohio	**US$** 991256.00

Chapter 17 - Cost and Freight

Abbreviation: CFR
Transport mode: vessel only
Contract type: shipment
Place: at the agreed port on the buyer's side

Cost and Freight (CFR) is another venerable shipment-delivery term. Its correct use should be generally limited to non-containerized waterborne shipments where the seller contracts for main carriage and handles vessel loading.

The concept of "ship's rail" has been dropped from the CFR rule. Sellers deliver the goods when they are on board the seller-appointed vessel. This is not as significant as it first appears, as A4 in both Incoterms 2000 and Incoterms® 2010 both say on board. Removal of the "ship's rail" phrase should not cause sellers undue anxiety as it is they who contract for main carriage. As "on board" is not defined, the parties should agree on exactly what this entails, particularly for charter movements.

A4 of the CFR rule contains another innovation by adding a provision covering goods that have already been delivered. This is intended to facilitate the use of this rule in commodity trade, where goods are commonly sold while in transit (so called "string sales").

CFR reflects the way most cargo was handled prior to containerization. Ports were little more than collections of piers to which outbound cargo was delivered. Nowadays, most modern ports are very secure areas. Outbound cargo is normally handed over some distance from the ships, and this is particularly true for containerized transportation. Still, there are instances where CFR is appropriate:

- with vessel chartering, where the seller handles vessel loading and main carriage, as is common in commodity trades or with break-bulk shipments of project cargo,
- when the goods are sold after they have been loaded,
- with containers at small or less developed ports.

Despite the fact that its correct use is limited, it is unlikely that the CFR Incoterms® rule will be deleted for many years to come. There are simply too many legacy issues.

Sellers should carefully contract for transportation to match the agreed point at the agreed place, since buyers are not required to reimburse them for any additional costs beyond that point. Since there is no consistency as to how and to whom carriers charge unloading and terminal handling costs at destination ports, the parties should address this in their sales contract and sellers should contract for transportation accordingly.

The CFR rule is used for shipment contracts as the seller delivers when the goods are loaded on the vessel for shipment within the agreed time frame to the agreed port. This seems counterintuitive at first as the place accompanying the rule is a port on the buyer's side of main carriage. However, it is at vessel loading that the seller's risk ends, not where the goods finally arrive .

The seller must also notify the buyer that the goods have been loaded so that the buyer can make arrangements to collect them.

International shipments are accommodated since sellers are responsible for export clearance.

Since the seller is contracting for carriage, it usually also appoints the forwarder for international transactions. This enables the seller to provide instructions to these parties without the risk of their following any conflicting instructions from the buyer.

BUYER-SELLER RESPONSIBILITIES

The following is a short list of responsibilities.

1. **Goods and Payment**
   The seller must contract for transportation for shipment within the agreed time frame. The buyer must pay the seller.
   Note: the packaging definition found in Incoterms® 2010[xxx] states that these rules do not cover container stowage and that this should be covered elsewhere in the sales contract. This is new.
2. **Loading and unloading**
   The seller is responsible for loading the goods onto the vessel.
3. **Pre-carriage and main carriage**
   Pre-carriage and contracting for and paying for main carriage are seller responsibilities under this rule.
4. **Export clearance**
   This is a seller responsibility under this rule.
5. **Other hoops and hurdles**
   The parties must work together on cargo security information. This usually means one party telling the other what is required and the other party providing it. Since security regulations change often and vary from country to country and from one transport mode to another, Incoterms® rules are limited to making the parties aware that they must be addressed. This is covered in A10-B10.
6. **Insurance**
   Neither party is required to insure under CFR. However, common sense dictates otherwise, and insurance should be addressed outside of the rule. Sellers bear the risk of loss until the goods are placed on board the vessel (check with your insurers about FAS/FOB coverage). Buyers are at risk thereafter.
7. **Documentary implications**
   a. Commercial Documents. The seller should provide a commercial invoice, a packing list, and any other commercial documents cited in the sales contract.

b. Transport Documents: The seller should provide evidence that the contract goods were loaded on the vessel. This should be an "on board" freight prepaid marine transport document.
c. Export Control Documentation: The seller is obligated to handle export clearance under both CFR and the Foreign Trade Regulations. With the possible exception of specific export licenses, there is no longer a paper document involved as U.S. export reporting is done electronically.
d. Import Entry Documentation: This is a buyer obligation. However, A10 requires the seller to provide assistance at the buyer's request, risk and cost.

8. **Payment terms considerations**

By definition, the seller must arrange for loading the goods onto the vessel. The only appropriate document would be one indicating that the goods are "on board." Since the seller is contracting for transportation, it would be freight prepaid. This document could easily be used to trigger a letter of credit. If negotiable (consigned to "order") it can also be used for documentary collections.

STORY LINE

None of the "usual suspects" would dream of using the CFR Incoterms® rule in day-to-day business. However, Glotz had some very large surplus equipment that was in good condition. It couldn't achieve the production economies needed for North America, but could be perfectly useful in a smaller market with lower labor costs. A Vietnamese manufacturer heard about it through a machinery broker and determined that it would suit his fledging operation.

As seen in Chapter 15, Glotz first quoted a price that included disassembling the equipment and transporting it to a Great Lakes port where they were able to obtain permission to bring it pier side. Then, the replacement for the intended vessel did not have a large enough crane, forcing Glotz to handle vessel loading shown in Chapter 16. However, the deal continued to deteriorate as the vessel was refused permission to enter the U.S. port. With its equipment already disassembled, packed and removed to the port, Glotz was forced to get further involved in the transportation. Fortunately, they found another tramp vessel in the Great Lakes with available space and bound for Vietnam. Glotz was able to subcharter space, but was required to pay the freight cost here. The parties agreed to have the letter of credit increased by $85,500 and amended to require a clean on board freight prepaid bill of lading rather than the freight collect document previously required. See proforma 17.1

AMERICAN VIEWPOINT

Quite a bit of cargo moves by chartered vessel in terms of tonnage. Bulk commodities are usually transported this way, although container imbalances have made U.S. produce exporters aware of the benefits of containers. Huge pieces of project cargo are transported by vessel. These shipments tend to be large and require detailed planning and execution by all parties. CFR works particularly well for products typically loaded by sellers from pier side facilities, such as liquids from tank farms, grain from elevators, etc.

International use

This Incoterms® rule tasks the seller with export clearance. For U.S. exporters, this is consistent with the Foreign Trade Regulations. The seller, known as the United States Principal Party in Interest (USPPI), is required to file the EEI or appoint an agent to do so, usually a seller-appointed forwarder. As the USPPI is contracting for transportation, it will have the necessary transportation information to file.

Bankers are quite attached to "on board ocean bills of lading."

For chartering, the fact that the seller selects the main carrier may not be so important for a purely volume consideration. Charter shipments are often negotiated individually, largely depending on vessel availability for the desired ports and times. However, for non-charter movements VOLUME is king, and sellers seeking large shipper status are helped by shipments on C-Group rules.

Experienced U.S. importers may prefer to buy on an F-Group rule unless their suppliers offer exceptionally attractive freight costs. If this is the case, consider holding the seller responsible for the carrier it chooses by requesting DAT or DAP rather than C-Group rules. In any case, insist on proof of what the freight costs are such as a rated transport document to avoid paying import duty on inbound freight costs.

Domestic use

Used correctly the CFR Incoterms® 2010 rule presents no problem for purely domestic transactions. Barge movements come to mind, and there is growing interest in "short-sea" shipments from one U.S. port to another.

[xxx] Incoterms®2010, (ISBN 978-92-842-0080-1), ICC No. 720, ICC Publishing SA, Paris, France, available from ICC Publishing Inc., New York, NY

PROFORMA INVOICE

EXPORTER Glotz Industries Inc 1492 Columbus Boulevard Fort Wayne, Indiana 12345-6789 USA	**PROFORMA INVOICE #** 17.1 **PROFORMA INVOICE DATE** December 13, 2010 **PROFORMA VALIDITY DATE** December 31, 2010 **EST'D SHIPMENT DATE** December 22, 2010
SOLD TO Vietnam Widgets Ltd. 4 Nixon Way Ho Chi Minh City VIETNAM	**TERMS OF PAYMENT** Irrevocable, confirmed letter of credit, payable at sight **SHIPMENT/DELIVERY TERMS** CFR Vung Tao Port, Vietnam, Incoterms 2010
SHIP TO Vung Tao Port, VIETNAM	**TITLE** Ownership transfers when payment is received by seller

QUANTITY	UNITS	DESCRIPTION OF MERCHANDISE	UNIT PRICE	TOTAL
1	Each	Used, complete widget manufacturing machine serial # 718-56, tested and operating at seller's premises before disassembly and shipment	973,500.00	973,500.00

LAW & DISPUTE RESOLUTION: The U.N. Convention on Contracts for the International Sale of Goods (1980) shall apply to this offer and any resulting contract. Any disputes will be resolved by binding arbitration services of the International Chamber of Commerce.	**MERCHANDISE TOTAL** Export Packing Pre-carriage to port Terminal handling Heavy lift & loading Forwarding Main carriage	**US$** 973500.00 7230.00 3192.00 625.00 6709.00 100.00 85500.00
	GRAND TOTAL CFR Vung Tao Port	**US$** 1,076,856.00

Chapter 18 - Cost Insurance and Freight

Abbreviation: CIF
Transport mode: vessel only
Contract type: shipment
Place: at the agreed port on the buyer's side

Cost Insurance and Freight (CIF) is another venerable shipment-delivery term. Its correct use should be generally limited to non-containerized waterborne shipments where the seller contracts for main carriage and handles vessel loading.

The concept of "ship's rail" has been dropped from the CIF rule. Sellers deliver the goods when they are on board the seller-appointed vessel. This is not as significant as it first appears, as A4 in both Incoterms 2000 and Incoterms® 2010 both say on board. Removal of the "ship's rail" phrase should not cause sellers undue anxiety as it is they who contract for main carriage. As "on board" is not defined, the parties should agree on exactly what this entails, particularly for charter movements.

A4 of the CIF rule contains another innovation by adding a provision covering goods that have already been delivered. This is intended to facilitate the use of this rule in commodity trade, where goods are commonly sold while in transit (so called "string sales").

CIF reflects the way most cargo was handled prior to containerization. Ports were little more than collections of piers to which outbound cargo was delivered. Nowadays, most modern ports are very secure areas. Outbound cargo is normally handed over some distance from the ships, and this is particularly true for containerized transportation. Still, there are instances where CIF is appropriate:

- with vessel chartering, where the seller handles vessel loading and main carriage, as is common in commodity trades or with break-bulk shipments of project cargo,
- when the goods are sold after they have been loaded,
- with containers at small or less developed ports.

Despite the fact that its correct use is limited, it is unlikely that the CIF Incoterms® rule will be deleted for many years to come. There are simply too many legacy issues.

Sellers should carefully contract for transportation to match the agreed point at the agreed place, since buyers are not required to reimburse them for any additional costs beyond that point. Since there is no consistency as to how and to whom carriers charge unloading and terminal handling costs at destination ports, the parties should address this in their sales contract and sellers should contract for transportation accordingly.

The CIF rule is used for shipment contracts as the seller delivers when the goods are loaded on the vessel for shipment within the agreed time frame to the agreed port. This seems counterintuitive at first as the place accompanying the rule is a port on the buyer's side of main carriage. However, it is at vessel loading that the seller's risk ends, not where the goods finally arrive.

The seller must also notify the buyer that the goods have been loaded so that the buyer can make arrangements to collect them.

International shipments are accommodated since sellers are responsible for export clearance.

Since the seller is contracting for carriage, it usually also appoints the forwarder for international transactions. This enables the seller to provide instructions to these parties without the risk of their following any conflicting instructions from the buyer.

The CIF rule stipulates that the seller must provide insurance, but limits this obligation to minimum cover unless the parties agree otherwise. Minimum cover is what we Americans call Free of Particular Average (FPA) and most others call Institute Cargo Clauses C. Either way, this coverage is extremely limited, and the parties should consider providing for additional risks for most shipments. **For the first time, such additional coverage is mentioned as an option in A3 of CIF. Also, specific Institute Cargo Clauses are mentioned.**

BUYER-SELLER RESPONSIBILITIES

The following is a short list of responsibilities.

1. **Goods and Payment**
   The seller must contract for transportation for shipment within the agreed time frame. The buyer must pay the seller.
   Note: the packaging definition found in Incoterms® 2010[xxxi] states that these rules do not cover container stowage and that this should be covered elsewhere in the sales contract. This is new.
2. **Loading and unloading**
   The seller is responsible for loading the goods onto the vessel.
3. **Pre-carriage and main carriage**
   Pre-carriage and contracting for and paying for main carriage are seller responsibilities under this rule.
4. **Export clearance**
   This is a seller responsibility under this rule.
5. **Other hoops and hurdles**
   The parties must work together on cargo security information. This usually means one party telling the other what is required and the other party providing it. Since security regulations change often and vary from country to country and from one transport mode to another, Incoterms® rules are limited to making the parties aware that they must be addressed. This is covered in A10-B10.
6. **Insurance**
   The seller is required to provide at least minimum cover insurance under CIF. Additional coverage should be considered.

7. **Documentary implications**
   a. Commercial Documents: The seller should provide a commercial invoice, a packing list, and any other commercial documents cited in the sales contract.
   b. Transport Documents: The seller should provide evidence that the contract goods were loaded on the vessel. This should be an "on board" freight prepaid marine transport document.
   c. Insurance Document: The seller should provide proof of insurance permitting the buyer or others with insurable interest to claim directly on the insurer.
   d. Export Control Documentation: The seller is obligated to handle export clearance under both CIF and the Foreign Trade Regulations. With the possible exception of specific export licenses, there is no longer a paper document involved as U.S. export reporting is done electronically.
   e. Import Entry Documentation: This is a buyer obligation. However, A10 requires the seller to provide assistance at the buyer's request, risk and cost.
8. **Payment terms considerations**
   By definition, the seller must arrange for loading the goods onto the vessel. The only appropriate document would be one indicating that the goods are "on board." Since the seller is contracting for transportation, it would be freight prepaid. This document could easily be used to trigger a letter of credit. If negotiable (consigned to "order") it can also be used for documentary collections.

STORY LINE

None of the "usual suspects" would dream of using the CIF Incoterms® rule in day-to-day business. However, Glotz had some very large surplus equipment that was in good condition. It couldn't achieve the production economies needed for North America, but could be perfectly useful in a smaller market with lower labor costs. A Vietnamese manufacturer heard about it through a machinery broker and determined that it would suit his fledging operation.

As seen in Chapter 17, a series of unforeseen events forced Glotz to get further in the transportation than they had anticipated. Glotz subchartered space on a Vietnam bound tramp vessel, but was required to pay the freight cost. The parties agreed to have the covering letter of credit increased by $85,500 and amended to require a clean on board freight prepaid bill of lading rather than the freight collect document previously required. Glotz then realized that they were at risk for the general average peril, so they and the buyer agreed to further increase the letter of credit and amend it to require an insurance certificate covering Institute Clauses A plus Strike and War Clauses. See proforma 18.1

AMERICAN VIEWPOINT

Quite a bit of cargo moves by chartered vessel in terms of tonnage. Bulk commodities are usually transported this way, although container imbalances have made U.S. produce exporters aware of the benefits of containers. Huge pieces of project cargo are transported on geared vessels (those equipped with lifting capability). These shipments tend to be large and require detailed planning and execution by all parties. CIF works particularly well for products typically loaded by sellers from pier side facilities, such as liquids from tank farms, grain from elevators, etc.

The best standard coverage is Institute Cargo Clauses A (LMA/IUA) or its equivalent. This is what we Americans mistakenly call "All Risks" (and really should call "Almost All Risks"). Whatever name you use, it should be enhanced by Strike, Riot and Civil Commotion coverage and War coverage. You may also want to consider having it written on a Warehouse to Warehouse basis, which is the insurance jargon equivalent for door-to-door. Note: The Institute Clauses were revised in 2009. Check what is and isn't included in these newly drafted clauses or their equivalent coverages with your insurer.

International use

This Incoterms® rule tasks the seller with export clearance. For U.S. exporters, this is consistent with the Foreign Trade Regulations. The seller, known as the United States Principal Party in Interest (USPPI), is required to file the EEI or appoint an agent to do so, usually a seller-appointed forwarder. As the USPPI is contracting for transportation, it will have the necessary transportation information to file.

Bankers are quite attached to "on board ocean bills of lading."

For chartering, the fact that the seller selects the main carrier may not be so important for a purely volume consideration. Charter shipments are often negotiated individually, largely depending on vessel availability for the desired ports and times. However, for non-charter movements VOLUME is king, and sellers seeking large shipper status are helped by shipments on C-Group rules.

Experienced U.S. importers may prefer to buy on an F-Group rule unless their suppliers offer exceptionally attractive freight costs. If this is the case, consider holding the seller responsible for the carrier it chooses by requesting DAT or DAP rather than C-Group rules. In any case, insist on proof of what the freight costs are such as a rated transport document to avoid paying import duty on inbound freight costs.

Domestic use

Used correctly the CIF Incoterms® 2010 rule presents no serious problem for purely domestic transactions. Barge movements come to mind, and there is growing interest in "short-sea" shipments from one U.S. port to another.

CIF does present a minor issue for domestic use, as most coverage for domestic shipments is written under what is called inland marine coverage. Unlike marine cargo insurance used for international shipments, inland marine is normally written to automatically cover all domestic shipments over an agreed period for a fixed premium. The policy holder normally claims in case of damage or loss. However, the CIF Incoterms® rule specifies that the buyer or other parties with insurable interest must be able to claim directly from the insurer. This can usually be addressed by a seller commitment to file any necessary claims in the buyer's behalf.

[xxxi] Incoterms®2010, (ISBN 978-92-842-0080-1), ICC No. 720, ICC Publishing SA, Paris, France, available from ICC Publishing Inc., New York, NY

PROFORMA INVOICE

EXPORTER Glotz Industries Inc 1492 Columbus Boulevard Fort Wayne, Indiana 12345-6789 USA	**PROFORMA INVOICE #** 18.1 **PROFORMA INVOICE DATE** December 14, 2010 **PROFORMA VALIDITY DATE** December 31, 2010 **EST'D SHIPMENT DATE** December 22, 2010
SOLD TO Vietnam Widgets Ltd. 4 Nixon Way Ho Chi Minh City VIETNAM	**TERMS OF PAYMENT** Irrevocable, confirmed letter of credit, payable at sight **SHIPMENT/DELIVERY TERMS** CIF Vung Tao Port, Vietnam, Incoterms 2010
SHIP TO Vung Tao Port, VIETNAM	**TITLE** Ownership transfers when payment is received by seller

QUANTITY	UNITS	DESCRIPTION OF MERCHANDISE	UNIT PRICE	TOTAL
1	Each	Used, complete widget manufacturing machine serial # 718-56, tested and operating at seller's premises before disassembly and shipment	973,500.00	973,500.00

LAW & DISPUTE RESOLUTION: The U.N. Convention on Contracts for the International Sale of Goods (1980) shall apply to this offer and any resulting contract. Any disputes will be resolved by binding arbitration services of the International Chamber of Commerce.

MERCHANDISE TOTAL	**US$** 973500.00
Export Packing	7230.00
Pre-carriage to port	3192.00
Terminal handling	625.00
Heavy lift & loading	6709.00
Forwarding	100.00
Main carriage	85500.00
Insurance (A+ War & Strike)	3661.31
GRAND TOTAL CIF Vung Tao Port	**US$** 1,080,517.31

Chapter 19 - An American Perspective

In keeping with this book's title, it is time to apply an American perspective both to Incoterms® rules in general and to Incoterms®2010[xxxii] in particular. We'll cover some new ground and provide more detail about some previously mentioned items of particular importance to us.

First, let's address the need for an American perspective. After all, Incoterms® 2010 rules are designed for worldwide use and are limited to business-to-business sales contracts for tangible goods. They indicate how sellers and buyers interact so that the seller should somehow get paid (B1) and to get the goods to the buyer (A1-A10 and B2-B10). Viewed that way, why this chapter?

Here are the reasons. There will be increasing use of Incoterms® 2010 rules in U.S. domestic trade now that we have a brand new revision (as of 2010). Next, while these rules broadly assign tasks, the ways the tasks are actually carried out vary from country to country. Just look at how our export control regulations amplify the general "export clearance" task. Finally, a given rule may result in consequences far beyond its intended scope. For instance, Incoterms® rules were not designed to address such issues as title transfer or revenue recognition, but other regulations use them as triggers for these purposes.

THE FORMER UNIFORM COMMERCIAL CODE TERMS

Until 2004, §2-319 through §2-324 of the Uniform Commercial Code (UCC) were devoted to terms of shipment and delivery. These were deleted as obsolete in 2004 as part of a massive revision of Article Two. Since commercial contracts are governed by state law, the revision was submitted to the states for their consideration. As of this writing (2010), few states have acted on the revision for two main reasons. UCC revisions are not politically exciting. More important, this huge UCC revision contains other issues which met with opposition from the United States Chamber of Commerce and the National Association of Manufacturers. While these are unrelated to the former shipment and delivery terms, they have contributed to holding up consideration by state legislatures. The net result is that the former UCC terms remain in the contract law of most states. Whether and when a significant number of states will embrace the revision is anyone's guess.

This writer was so sure that the UCC revision would catch on quickly that he coauthored a book and launched a series of seminars about converting domestic business from UCC to Incoterms® rules. The results were surprising. A number of rather large U.S. companies expressed strong interest in using Incoterms® rules for their domestic transactions for their own convenience, regardless of whether their state's law had changed. These companies typically engage in exports and imports as well in domestic transactions. The practice of juggling two sets of terms between international and domestic operations is both inefficient and confusing – all the more so as some have similar abbreviations but entirely different meanings.

This approach makes sense. We Americans enjoy significant freedom of contract. There's no problem with using Incoterms® rules in domestic transactions, provided the parties clearly indicate that they are doing so. As mentioned in Chapter Four, the preferred method of doing so is to cite the rule, the place, and Incoterms® 2010 (such as CIP 1150 South McCord Rd, Holland, Ohio, USA, Incoterms® 2010). Be sure to follow this procedure. Failure to indicate that you are using an Incoterms® rule could result in the application of an old UCC term by default in case of a dispute.

A major reason why we hadn't seen a significant movement to domestic use as of this writing was expectation of the 2010 revision. No one wanted to change to a soon-to-be-obsolete set of rules, and the recent average lifespan of an Incoterms® version is 10 years. Now, the brand new and thoroughly revised 2010 Incoterms® rules provide an excellent point of departure. We predict a major shift, probably lead by large companies requesting all their materials suppliers to use Incoterms® 2010 rules. This should prompt these suppliers to ask the same of their vendors, and so on. Consider the e-commerce ripple effect that the Detroit Big Three caused twenty years ago by requiring their direct suppliers to communicate with them electronically.

CONVERSION FROM THE FORMER UCC SHIPMENT AND DELIVERY TERMS TO INCOTERMS® 2010

Now that we've seen why the former UCC terms will decline in favor of Incoterms® 2010 rules for domestic trade, let's see how to get there. As we are covering domestic use, we won't consider export or import clearance. Also, since the old UCC terms have been imbedded in state laws, I need to recite my usual disclaimer about this not being construed as legal advice.

UCC §2-319 covered the former Free On Board (F.O.B.) term, which was by far the most widely used and least understood. Its popularity came from the fact that it was twisted to fit every conceivable situation, with the result that FOB used by itself meant nothing. For it to make sense, one had to specify both the place and which party was contracting for carriage. By contrast, Incoterms® 2010 rules also require a place but themselves indicate which party contracts for carriage. Also, the UCC F.O.B. term could be used for either shipment or arrival contracts. Again by contrast, each Incoterms® 2010 rule clearly indicates this through the delivery point in A4-B4.

Both UCC F.O.B. and F.A.S. were covered together in §2-319. We'll start with the F.O.B. permutations.

Former UCC F.O.B. origin, freight collect: This is probably what we thought we meant when we used our beloved "FOB Factory," The seller was responsible for having the goods available at the place where the shipment originated, with no carriage obligation. Delivery occurred at the origin place. However, the seller had no obligation to load the collecting vehicle. The appropriate Incoterms® 2010 rule matchup is Ex Works (EXW), where the seller also has no carriage obligation and delivers at the origin place. It would at first seem that FCA accompanied by the origin place would also match, but it doesn't, as FCA obligates the seller to load the collecting vehicle. Like EXW, this old UCC term had limited real life application since sellers usually do load collecting vehicles. This term would work with small package carriers where the drivers actually load their own trucks. Another possibility would be with customers who pick up goods in their own vehicles and are willing to load them.

Both the UCC term and the EXW Incoterms® 2010 rule are intended for use in shipment contracts for all modes of transportation.

Former UCC F.O.B. origin, car or other vehicle, freight collect: This holds the seller responsible for loading. The seller had no carriage obligations, and delivered by loading the collecting vehicle. The seller's loading obligation clearly matches this to FCA when accompanied by the origin place.

Both the UCC term and the FCA Incoterms® 2010 rule are intended for use in shipment contracts for all modes of transportation.

Former UCC F.O.B. origin, freight prepaid: The seller contracted for carriage but delivered by handing over the goods to the carrier. This is an excellent matchup for either CPT or CIP, depending on whether the seller insures. As mentioned in Chapter Six, there needs to be some tweaking if CIP is used, as under the Incoterms® 2010 rule the buyer or anyone with insurable interest should be able to claim directly from the insurer. Since this is not the way inland marine coverage normally works, the parties should agree that the seller will claim against its policy on the buyer's behalf.

Both the UCC term and the CPT and CIP Incoterms® rules are intended for use in shipment contracts for all modes of transportation.

Former UCC F.O.B. destination, freight collect: The seller had no carriage obligation but remained responsible for the condition of the goods until they arrived. There is no matching Incoterms® rule, and a moment's thought will reveal why. As carriage was contracted by the buyer, how could the seller claim for in-transit damage? What if the buyer used its own truck? Would the seller nevertheless remain responsible for the condition of the goods until they arrive?

This UCC term was intended for use in arrival contracts for all modes of transportation.

Former UCC F.O.B. destination, freight prepaid: The seller was responsible for carriage and delivered when the goods arrived. This is a matchup for the new Incoterms® 2010 rule, Delivered At Place (DAP). In both situations, the seller contracts for carriage and is responsible for the performance of the carrier as delivery occurs at arrival. Incidentally, this new Incoterms® 2010 rule specifically addresses the need for an omnimodal import-clearance-neutral rule for domestic arrival contracts. Under Incoterms 2000[xxxiii], there was only Delivered Duty Unpaid (DDU) and Delivered Duty Paid (DDP), either of which caused problems with domestic sales of pre-imported goods.

Both the UCC term and the DAP Incoterms® 2010 rule are intended for use in arrival contracts for all modes of transportation.

Former UCC F.O.B. vessel: This matched the 2010 Incoterms® FOB rule pretty well. One exception is that the Incoterms® 2010 rule provides for string sales. Another is that the UCC term specified that unless otherwise agreed, the buyer must make payment against the required documents, and that the goods themselves were not acceptable substitute for the documents. By contrast, B1 of Incoterms® 2010 rules simply states that the buyer must pay the price, without specifying when or how.

Both the UCC term and the FOB Incoterms® 2010 rule are intended for use in shipment contracts, and are designed for waterborne transportation.

The other former UCC shipment and delivery terms were far less frequently used, mainly because the F.O.B. term was twisted around to fit all situations. Also, savvy international traders have long ago abandoned the UCC terms in favor of Incoterms® 2010 rules for their international transactions. Finally, as we will see, there are some former UCC terms which make little sense in today's world.

Former UCC §2-319 covered Free Alongside (F.A.S.) along with F.O.B. The matchup with F.A.S. was pretty close to the 2010 Free Alongside Ship (FAS) Incoterms® rule except as mentioned in the former UCC F.O.B. vessel term above.

Both the UCC term and the FAS Incoterms® 2010 rule are intended for use in shipment contracts and are designed for waterborne transportation.

Former UCC §2-320 Cost, Insurance and Freight (C.I.F.) and Cost & Freight (C. & F.): As with F.O.B. and F.A.S., the UCC covered the C.I.F. and C. & F. terms together in the same part. It defined C.I.F. and explained C. & F. as an exception to the insurance requirement. In both terms, the seller contracted for carriage to the agreed port on the buyer's side, but delivered by loading the vessel at the port on the seller's side. These match up reasonably well with the individual CIF and CFR Incoterms® 2010 rules. As mentioned above, one exception is that the Incoterms® 2010 rules provide for string sales. Another is that the UCC terms specified that unless otherwise agreed, the buyer must make payment against the required documents, and that the goods themselves were not acceptable substitute for the documents. By contrast, B1 of all Incoterms® 2010 rules simply states that the buyer must pay the price, without specifying when or how.

Both the UCC terms and the CIF and CFR Incoterms® 2010 rules are intended for use in shipment contracts and are designed for waterborne transportation.

Former UCC §2-321 Cost, Insurance and Freight (C.I.F.) and Cost & Freight (C. & F.) Net Landed Weights: This UCC term was odd, so please bear with me. Take the former C.I.F. or C. & F., and add the further seller responsibility for the arrived weight or quantity of the contract goods. The seller would weigh the shipment, and ship under either the C.I.F. or C. & F. term. If the weight or quantity was lower on arrival, the seller would be responsible for the difference. If miraculously the weight or quantity increased in transit, the seller would gain the difference. (Presumably, there were mechanisms in place to deal with increased weight through moisture accumulation common with vessel shipments.) There are no corresponding Incoterms® 2010 rules, and a moment's thought should provide the reason. Both C.I.F. and C. & F. were for use in shipment contracts where the seller delivered by loading the vessel. If the entire ship sunk, or the shipment were jettisoned, the seller had zero responsibility for the goods. How would it logically follow for the seller to be responsible for a mere shortage?

The answer is that Incoterms® 2010 rules do not operate this way. Instead, they focus on "Delivery," which is precisely covered in A4-B4 of all rules. Once the seller delivers, its responsibility ends as cited in A5-B5 "Transfer of Risks" of all rules.

Former UCC §2-322 Delivery Ex Ship (D.E.S.): The seller contracted for carriage and remained responsible for the condition of the goods until they were unloaded from the vessel at the agreed port on the buyer's side. This matches up with the new Incoterms® 2010 rule Delivered At Terminal (DAT) when the place specified with the rule is the quay at the named destination port.

Both the UCC term and the DAT Incoterms® 2010 rule are intended for use in arrival contracts. The UCC term was designed for waterborne transportation, while DAT may be used for all transport modes.

Former UCC §2-323 Bill of Lading: Although placed among the former UCC shipment and delivery terms, Part 2-323 described a bill of lading document. Nowhere in Incoterms® 2010 is a bill of lading described.

Former UCC §2-324 No Arrival, No Sale: This was another strange UCC term for which there is no matching Incoterms® rule. It was used for arrival contracts, and gave the seller an escape if the contract goods failed to arrive because of reasons beyond the seller's control. It also refers to UCC §2-613 Casualty to Identified Goods which has not been deleted from the UCC. Besides terminating the contract in case of total loss, this addresses partial loss or damage by allowing the buyer to either terminate the contract or accept the goods at reduced pricing but without further rights against the seller.

As we saw in UCC §2-321 above, Incoterms® 2010 rules do not work this way. Instead, they focus on "Delivery," which is precisely covered in A4-B4 of all rules. Once the seller delivers, its responsibility ends as cited in A5-B5 "Transfer of Risks" of all rules.

STRETCHING

As mentioned in the Caveat section of Chapter 4, we must avoid stretching an Incoterms® 2010 rule beyond its intended scope. Americans unfamiliar with Incoterms® 2010 rules have a tendency to try using an F-Group term accompanied by a final destination in an arrival contract. This comes from the "F.O.B. destination" variations of the former UCC F.O.B. term described earlier.

Since the FOB Incoterms® 2010 rule is used only for waterborne transport, there is only one possible place: on a ship at a port on the seller's side. Same for the FAS Incoterms® 2010 rule, except that the only possible place is next to a ship at a port on the seller's side. These two rules are used in shipment contracts. They should never be used with other places.

The omnimodal FCA rule comes in two flavors, either

a. at the seller's premises (i.e. the place where shipment begins before any carriage)
   or
b. somewhere else on the seller's side after pre-carriage but before any main carriage (often a buyer-appointed carrier's terminal or forwarder's warehouse).

It is used in shipment contracts in alternative "a," as the seller delivers at its premises merely by loading the goods onto a buyer-appointed carrier. FCA is also used for shipment contracts in alternative "b." Although the seller delivers when the goods arrive at the specified place, it must always be at the seller's side of some subsequent transportation (main carriage) because A3 states that the seller has no carriage obligation.

Therefore, the only time it would be appropriate for Americans to use EXW or an F-Group Incoterms® 2010 rule with a foreign place would be when the shipment begins there. One example would be sales of goods from a foreign location, such as happens with imports. Another would be local overseas sales of pre-exported U.S. goods from an overseas warehouse. (The overseas warehouse would be the place of shipment, and the costs paid to get them there would presumably have already been folded into the selling price of the goods themselves.)

We have been using the expression "seller's side" and "buyer's side" for convenience, as they do play out nicely in international trade. The seller's side would be in the seller's country, on the seller's side of main carriage. The buyer's side would be another country (often the buyer's) on the other side of main carriage. Since we are now considering the use of Incoterms® 2010 rules in domestic trade, we can get away from the countries and simply think in terms of the seller's side of main carriage or the buyer's side of main carriage. When there is only one carrier, as is often the case with domestic shipments, the issue becomes even simpler. It's the seller's side of carriage or the buyer's side of carriage. However, as mentioned above, FCA A3 specifies that the seller is not responsible for carriage, so that place used with FCA should not be the final destination. Instead, DAP has been designed for use in both domestic and international freight-paid arrival contracts.

The converse to stretching is equally true but is nowhere near as widespread. The place with C-Group and D-Group terms should always be somewhere on the buyer's side, as the seller is contracting for carriage to get the goods there.

INCOTERMS®2010 RULES AND TITLE

This issue comes up again, again and again. The simple answer is that Incoterms® 2010 rules do not address title passage. OK, then what does? Answer: either the sales contract or, failing that, applicable law.

The most logical approach is also the most obvious. Sellers and buyers should agree to when, where and how title passes in their sales contract. Where in the contract? Anywhere except the selected Incoterms® 2010 rule. Some possible transfer points include: "upon shipment," "upon arrival," "upon payment," "upon withdrawal from inventory" (for consignment goods), "the fourth full moon of the year," or just about anywhere else the parties agree. Some countries may have restrictive law on this, but many embrace reasonable freedom of contract.

OK, what happens if it isn't specified? Probably nothing, unless there is a dispute. However, if title passage becomes contentious and the contract is silent, it becomes an issue for the applicable law.

UCC §2-401 was not removed in the 2004 revision and appears more or less the same in the contract law of most U.S. states. It states that for contracts not specifying otherwise, ownership passes when the seller delivers. Incoterms® rules do speak to delivery in A4-B4. Does this mean that the Incoterms® 2010 rule determines when ownership passes? No. What the Incoterms® 2010 rule states about delivery may trigger title passage by default if the contract is silent and the governing law says so. It's the law, not the Incoterms® 2010 rule.

Why not redesign the Incoterms® 2010 rules to cover title passage? Several reasons. Laws about ownership differ from country to country. The law that governs much international trade, the United Nations Convention on Contracts for the International Sale of Goods (CISC), doesn't address ownership passage at all. Also, the simplest reason is that Incoterms® 2010 rules speak to shipment and delivery, and one can possess goods without owning them, or own goods without possessing them. (Finance your car?)

If I managed to get this one point across, you are miles ahead of the pack.

FOREIGN TRADE REGULATIONS

As mentioned in the Caveat section of Chapter 4, the Census Bureau Foreign Trade Division imposed revised export reporting rules shortly after Incoterms 2000 was released, and again in June 2008. They are found in 15 CFR Part 30 Foreign Trade Regulations (FTR).

Under these regulations, the U.S. seller is called the United States Principal Party in Interest (USPPI). The foreign buyer is called the Foreign Principal Party in Interest (FPPI). The changes also brought the concept of "routed transactions." Part 303.3(e) defines a routed transaction as "a transaction in which the FPPI authorizes a U.S. agent to facilitate the export of items from the United States and to prepare and file EEI (Electronic Export Information)." Normally, this would mean a buyer-appointed forwarder. (As the line between carrier and forwarder is now quite blurry, it could also be a carrier acting as a forwarder or a forwarder acting as a carrier). In any event, the operative phrase is buyer-appointed, which usually means EXW, FCA, FAS and FOB Incoterms® 2010 rules.

This seems to work well with the EXW rule, as the seller is not obligated to arrange for export clearance. However, the government has made it clear that it will hold all parties potentially responsible for any export violation, and that the seller cannot escape its obligations as USPPI by merely invoking the EXW Incoterms® 2010 rule.

In a routed transaction, under FTR §30.3(e)(1), the USPPI must provide the following information to the authorized U.S. agent of the FPPI:

- USPPI's name and address
- USPPI's EIN
- State of origin
- Schedule B descriptions
- Schedule B numbers
- Origin of goods indicator (D or F)
- Quantity / units of measure
- Value
- ECCN or other U.S. government agencies' license identifiers
- Sufficient technical information to determine the U.S. government licensing authority.

The conflict between the FTR and Incoterms® 2010 rules is with FCA, FAS and FOB which hold sellers responsible for export clearance. As with EXW, the USPPI must provide the FPPI's agent with the above information so the agent can submit the EEI. Fortunately, the FTR offers a remedy. The FPPI can appoint the USPPI as an agent to file the EEI in its behalf. To do so, the FPPI would issue a power of attorney or other written authorization to the USPPI. Armed with this authorization, the USPPI would require the buyer-appointed forwarder to provide the shipment-specific information to enable the USPPI to complete and file the EEI. The FPPI should be happy to do so. After all, by using an F-Group rule the parties have already agreed that the USPPI is to handle export clearance. Further, chances are that the USPPI would not charge for doing this, while a buyer-appointed forwarder almost certainly would. In fact, the only drawback to this solution is that such EEIs must be filed pre-departure.

As a conscientious exporter I prefer to file my own EEIs than trust them to a forwarder I didn't select and over which I have no control. I also have an ulterior motive. As a reasonably well informed exporter, I prefer to control main carriage whenever possible. I always start an export relationship by quoting on the seller-friendly C-Group rules. I don't always get my way, and sometimes wind up dealing with buyer appointed carriers and forwarders – a situation not to my liking. By forcing the buyer-appointed forwarder to provide the transportation specific information, I can help my forwarder seek lower freight costs and better service to capture control of future deals.

EXPORT LICENSE REQUIREMENTS

Sometimes, export licenses are issued with the condition that the exporter obtain delivery verification to ensure that the goods are actually received by the approved party. Obviously, sellers in these circumstances should insist on Incoterms® 2010 rules that enable them to contract for carriage (C and D-Group). Sellers of goods subject to tight export controls might consider this as a general practice even for shipments where delivery verification is not specifically required. Knowing when, where and to whom the carrier released a shipment of a tightly controlled item can help avoid sleepless nights. Naturally, one must be in a position to give the carrier such instructions, which means contracting with it as in C-Group and D-Group Incoterms® 2010 rules.

REVENUE RECOGNITION

By revenue recognition we mean at what point a sale can be considered an account receivable. This is an important accounting issue, particularly for publicly traded U.S. corporations anxious to satisfy shareholders by exceeding Wall Street analysts' expectations. This means getting financial statements as strong as possible at the close of accounting periods. Revenue recognition regulations have been around for some time, and the Securities and Exchange Commission (www.sec.gov) regulates publicly traded corporations. What has changed is the increased penalties for accounting irregularities imposed by Sarbanes-Oxley (SOX). CEOs and CFOs have become very scrupulous in their insistence that accounting regulations be closely followed.

Revenue recognition rules are not limited to the SEC. The Financial Accounting Standards Board's Generally Accepted Accounting Principles (GAAP) standards for reporting financial information also speak to revenue recognition. Internationally, the International Financial Reporting Standards (IFRS) are becoming the national GAAP for such countries as Canada, China and Russia. The SEC is now accepting financial statements prepared under IFRS from foreign private issuers of securities as a substitute for those prepared under U.S. GAAP.

Delivery as used in Incoterms® 2010 rules is a factor in these regulations and standards. Revenue recognition concern can influence the choice of an Incoterms® rule, particularly for publicly traded corporations anxious to recognize it as early as possible. D-Group Incoterms® 2010 rules hold that delivery happens at arrival, usually after all or most of the transportation, therefore delaying revenue recognition. This may put publicly traded U.S. firms at a competitive disadvantage against foreign competition which may not be similarly regulated.

Sometimes, an Incoterms® 2010 rule isn't sufficient to satisfy an auditor that delivery took place. I have a firsthand example of a client that had recently become publicly traded and was under strong Wall Street pressure to perform. They manufactured a small product, and frequently received a flurry of orders at month end. They wanted to use the EXW rule and deliver by having the shipments available on their loading dock and notifying their customers, even late at night after their carrier's usual pickup time. Their auditor objected, asking what would happen if the building burned down that night. I do not know the outcome, and mention this to illustrate what unintended consequences can attach to Incoterms® rules.

[xxxii] Incoterms® 2010, (ISBN 978-92-842-0080-1), ICC No. 720, ICC Publishing SA, Paris, France, available from ICC Publishing Inc., New York, NY
[xxxiii] Incoterms 2000 (ISBN 92-842-1199-9), ICC No. 560, ICC Publishing SA, Paris, France, available from ICC Publishing Inc., New York, NY

Chapter 20 - How Incoterms® Rules Relate to Everything Else

This chapter is really the reason you've waded through this book. It contains some "cheat sheets" that outline the various characteristics of Incoterms® 2010 rules from different perspectives. However, it comes with a big warning. **IT DOES NOT STAND ALONE.** In order to avoid becoming misled, you must have already read the previous 19 chapters.

ICC GROUPINGS

As explained in the Introduction to Incoterms® 2010[xxxiv], the rules are first separated into omnimodal and marine-only groups, and then listed in terms of increasing seller cost, risk and responsibility. This is an improvement, as it helps users avoid incorrectly applying marine-only rules. However, it does break up the continuous progression found in former Incoterms® versions. We'll restore the original perspective by listing the new rules the former way. We'll also preserve the improvement by stating each rule's appropriate use right next to it.

E DEPARTURE
EXW – place from which shipment begins (usually seller's premises) – omnimodal (really non-modal)

F-GROUP - MAIN CARRIAGE UNPAID
FCA – either from which the shipment begins (usually seller's premises) or another place on the seller's side of main (or subsequent) carriage – omnimodal
FAS – alongside a vessel at a port on the seller's side – marine-restricted
FOB – on a vessel at a port on the seller's side – marine-restricted

C-GROUP - MAIN CARRIAGE PAID
CPT – an agreed place on the buyer's side of carriage – omnimodal
CIP – an agreed place on the buyer's side of carriage – omnimodal
CFR – a port on the buyer's side of carriage – marine restricted
CIF – a port on the buyer's side of carriage – marine restricted

D-GROUP - ARRIVAL
DAT – a terminal on the buyer's side of carriage – omnimodal
DAP – an agreed place (other than a terminal) on the buyer's side of carriage – omnimodal
DDP – an agreed place on the buyer's side of carriage – omnimodal

This original Incoterms® presentation reinforces a point we've seen throughout this book. FCA's presence in the "main carriage unpaid" group shows how inappropriate it would be for use with a final destination.

EXPORT-IMPORT CLEARANCE IRREGULARITIES

The following two terms are unique from all others. Neither work well in practice, at least for Americans. Both have one party attempting to comply with regulations of the other party's country.

EXW is the only Incoterms® 2010 rule that makes export clearance a buyer obligation. As we've seen countless times, it doesn't work well in practice at least for Americans.

DDP is the only Incoterms® 2010 rule that makes import clearance a seller obligation. It creates a high level of risk for American sellers. Although possible for American buyers, it may give rise to increased risk-related pricing and otherwise avoidable clearance delays, and is awkward for drawback situations.

With all other rules, the seller is responsible for export clearance and the buyer is responsible for import clearance.

PAYMENT TERM MATCHUP

We've seen this with each individual rule, but an overview is useful. The following is not exhaustive. Payment instruments like documentary credits can be structured to provide for many different kinds of trigger documents. Standby credits normally require only beneficiary certifications rather than shipping documents, so we will not consider them here. Documentary collections rely on the buyer's inability to access the goods without first paying or accepting a draft at a bank. As this is usually controlled by a transport document, it can be important which party controls the issuer which is almost always a carrier or freight forwarder.

We'll use the following abbreviations:
COD = cash on delivery
D/C = documentary collection
L/C = documentary letter of credit
O/A = open account
W/O = with order (we'll not abbreviate "cash in advance" for obvious reasons).
We'll also use the earlier Incoterms® lineup to illustrate the seller's cost, risk, responsibility.

EXW – W/O or O/A

FCA – W/O, O/A, possibly L/C (payable against freight collect truck bill of lading, forwarder's receipt, or freight collect received-for-shipment multimodal transport document), or D/C with negotiable freight collect received-for-shipment multimodal transport document. COD is also remotely possible if the place is other than the seller's premises.

FAS – W/O, O/A, possibly L/C (payable against either a mate's receipt, a dock receipt, or remotely possible with a freight collect received-for-shipment multimodal transport document), D/C remotely possible with a negotiable freight collect received-for-shipment multimodal transport document). FAS is not normally used with multimodal transportation.

FOB – W/O, O/A, L/C, D/C
CPT – W/O, O/A, L/C (should call for a received-for-shipment prepaid transport document), D/C
CIP – W/O, O/A, L/C (should call for a received-for-shipment prepaid transport document), D/C
CFR – W/O, O/A, L/C (should call for an on board prepaid marine transport document), D/C
CIF – W/O, O/A, L/C (should call for an on board prepaid marine transport document), D/C
DAT – W/O, O/A, L/C (should call for a terminal-issued document), D/C (negotiable terminal document?)
DAP – WO, O/A, L/C (if prepaid shipping document is acceptable to buyer), D/C (same as L/C)
DDP – WO/O/A, L/C (if prepaid shipping and duty paid customs entry documents are acceptable to buyer).
Note: The D-Group rules hold the seller responsible for arrival, while shipping documents prove only that shipment has been made.

USEFULNESS TO AMERICANS

With the exception of EXW and DDP, all Incoterms®2010 rules are useful in international trade, although some are more restricted than others. The same is true for domestic trade, and even EXW can work here for carriers that load their own conveyances.

FCA: is by far the most versatile of the F-Group rules. It can conceivably be used for all main carriage unpaid situations by merely adjusting the accompanying place: at the seller's premises, loaded on a truck, at a carrier's terminal or forwarder's warehouse, next to a ship, even on a ship. However, custom dies hard. There are many contracts specifying the marine-only rules. Also, there is resistance in trade finance to "received-for-shipment" documentation, often to the point of forcing sellers to exceed their FCA obligations by requiring on-board documentation. Some day, there will be one F-Group rule, but not yet.

FAS: this is normally used for charter movements.

FOB: Should be normally used for charter movements but for the on-board document preference. It imposes significant additional risk for sellers using containers with scheduled ship lines. The seller remains responsible for vessel loading onto a vessel by a carrier with which it has no contractual relationship at a port which it probably cannot even enter.

CPT: is another versatile rule which is appropriate for all modes of transport when on-board documentation is not required. However, buyers need to beware of the "first carrier" situation and either specify a different delivery point or provide adequate warehouse-to-warehouse insurance coverage. Sellers should contract for transportation only to the agreed point, and the parties should agree to destination cost distribution beforehand.

CIP: As with CPT except that seller insures and the parties should consider additional coverage.

CFR: Works well for vessel shipments where on-board documentation is required. Sellers should have no problem with loading vessels of their own choosing. Parties should agree to what "on-board" means as the traditional ship's rail has been removed from the rule. Sellers should contract for transportation only to the agreed point, and the parties should agree to destination cost distribution beforehand.

CIF: As with CFR except that seller insures and the parties should consider additional coverage.

DAT: This new omnimodal term is the only rule specifically tasking the seller with unloading. Useful for all modes when buyers pick up at carriers' terminals and provide any required on-carriage.

DAP: This omnimodal successor to DDU is extremely useful, particularly now that the "duty unpaid" is removed from the name to avoid complication in domestic sales of pre-imported goods. Sellers should contract for transportation only to the agreed point, and the parties should agree to destination cost distribution beforehand.

DDP: This omnimodal rule makes as little sense as ever for Americans, except where the seller is willing to take extraordinary measures to avoid any buyer inconvenience. The mere fact that it is possible to do something doesn't argue that doing so makes commercial sense.

[xxxiv] Incoterms® 2010, (ISBN 978-92-842-0080-1), ICC No. 720, ICC Publishing SA, Paris, France, available from ICC Publishing Inc., New York, NY

Index